MY POETRY WELL

MY POETRY WELL

(Lower Your Buckets For Treasures)

Elliot Thaul

iUniverse, Inc.
New York Lincoln Shanghai

MY POETRY WELL
(Lower Your Buckets For Treasures)

Copyright © 2008 by Elliot Thaul

iUniverse books may be ordered through booksellers or by contacting:

iUniverse
2021 Pine Lake Road, Suite 100
Lincoln, NE 68512
www.iuniverse.com
1-800-Authors (1-800-288-4677)

ISBN: 978-0-595-48732-5 (pbk)
ISBN: 978-0-595-60825-6 (ebk)

Printed in the United States of America

Contents

Preface

I've been writing poetry for most of my 91 years.

My style is to use everyday conversational words that do not require the use of a dictionary. Each poem is usually written in meter and rhyme without esoteric language.

Since being named Poet Laureate of the Berkshire Writers Room Inc., I've decided to share some of my favorite poems with others.

Hope you enjoy reading them.

Elliot Thaul

My Poetry Well

Come! Lower your buckets—
And you will find
Treasures
Of every kind.

POETRY
May I Pour You Some?

like
some
rare
aging
bottled
wine, – chance
selected sub-
conscious ideas
percolate, fer-
ment, – and then
emerge shaped in
measured meter
for bottling as
vintaged verse
labeled POETRY!

(1996)

A Friendly Smile

I smiled as I was passing by
And caught the glimmer in her eye.
She sat upon a folding chair.
Of wrinkled face and long gray hair—
Her gaze gripped mine and locked it there.
She seemed to question—WHY!?
I turned and smiled again.
Her frail thin body straightened high!
And LO!—as though of Queenly Reign—
She Beamed—and—waived Her Royal Cane!

Her warmth lit up my heart That Day!
Just a simple smile in a simple way.

(1995)

A HALLOWEEN TALE—2002

The Witches flew in with their screaming bats.
They parked their brooms and hung their hats.
'Twas the night before Halloween.
Witches galore were on the scene
Rehearsing roles in shadowy light—
With shrieks and howls—all kids to fright.

But,—the kids were prepared!—On Halloween night—
'Twas they who scared the Witches.—What a sight!
They pelted them with apples, pumpkins and pies.
Trembling Witches soon darkened the skies.
The kids then loosed caged alley cats—
That gave speedy chase to flapping bats.
Hard nuts, gum balls, candy,—and more tiny bits—
Were hurled at the Witches—now out of their wits.
Oh,—how they cackled!—Oh,—how they tried!—
But their plans all fizzled.—FLEE!—they all cried.
Loose black capes, slapping in the winds,—
Spanked them soundly for their Devilish sins.
When suddenly, in formation, they all took flight—
And disappeared into the moonlit night.

Of course, watching were proud Mom and Dad.
What a glorious time everyone had!
The kids rang doorbells:—'Trick or Treat!"
And refilled their bags with goodies to eat.
To add more cheer,—they played harmless pranks—
Then gathered to Party—to give Joyous thanks.
In full spirit of Fun and Friendship galore—
All pledged to celebrate Halloween forever more
With parades and music and dance—as never before.
Whee!—screamed the kiddies—as happy as could be.

(2002)

(Prepared for Pittsfield 'Art In The Park' Halloween Poetry reading Oct.
4,2002)

Alzheimer's?

If I could only remember—
But,—I forget—and—forget!
Did I sin?
When did it begin?
It's so demeaning—
When you fumble for a name,—
Or,—when you're driving:—"Whither To?"—
I thought I knew.
Nothing is the same.
Who is that face?
A stranger?—A friend?
Is there no end?
All those stares and smiles?
Why?
Who am I?
Where am I?
Hello Jimmy—My son!
Don't run!
Oh No!—Silly me,—
I didn't see.
And You—you are John,—my darling husband?
Please kiss me!
Who Are You Sir!?
Do I know you?
All is a blur!
No!—I'm not crazy!
Everything seems so hazy.
Is this the Present?—the Past?
How long will it last?
Please!—Please!—DON'T LEAVE ME!!
I'm scared—and—so tired!

(1998)

4

Aging Memories

As we age—

    In our old cage,—
        Today's scenes slip by
           Our weakened eye.

Alas!—Time spins too fast—
    Blurring echoes of the past.

Listen to the Pendulum!
    It sings our weary song
Of fond memories once strong.
    While you can—RECORD them!
Make Haste!—
    'Ere they're forgotten—
And gone to waste.

(2000)

Almost?

Life is a challenge of reaching goals!
Like riding a galloping horse on a Carousel,—
We see our prize,—
But always just beyond our reach.
We all ride the Carousel—
—Life's Merry-Go-Round of Dreams!

(2002)

A Morning In The Berkshires

I saw the Berkshire morning mist—
So many wisps of spray—
Like loosened balls of cotton
To bathe the newborn day.

Floating—weightless wafers—
Ever downward bound—slowly paced
'Til their seamless—shapeless bodies
Softly touched and interlaced.

Oh!—What a sight to behold!

I saw a milky blanket—
As tho brushed by unseen hand—
Painting rolling hills and valleys
Of our treasured Berkshire land.

I saw stretching—sparkling grasses
Laden full with morning dew—
Gently dripping clustered jewels
'Neath the skyline's breaking blue.

Soon—waking rays of Summer's Sun
Warmly kissed the morning mist
To fold it once again away
For yet another Berkshire Day.

(1993)

AN ODE TO MY BARBER

Listen to the music of the Barber's sound—
As his scissors and comb go 'round and 'round.
Up and down—dance his waving hands—
Like Conductors leading some unseen bands—
With a comb-snip here and a comb-snip there—
Cutting clutches of growing hair.
I thrill to the rhythm of his scissors' click—
Tho un-nerved at times to an errant nick.
Expectant?—Yes!—But,—it never comes.
We gab a lot.—He even hums—
And flashes a most warming grin
When he talks about his mandolin.
Like an Artist sculpting with steady hand—
He shapes my crown on a revolving stand.
Then,—with a mirror behind my skull—
He calls:—"YOU'RE NEXT!!—THANKS!—THAT'S ALL!!

(1998)

A Plea—1995

Tombstones and Crosses in rows all abound
Where grasses and flowers ought to be found.
Fields of clover where children would play
Are covered with mounds where dead flowers lay.

Such is the mood! Morality gone wild!
Ethnic greed by Witches beguiled!
Seething masses,—uprooted,—torn,—
Trudging of Death in despair,—Forlorn!

Peoples of the World—Hearken!
Give up All Hate!
Else the Globe will darken—
And seal All Fate!

I call upon You—Satan!
Ease up thy Sword!
Make room for the Sun—
And Peaceful Accord!

(1995)

A Plea For Goodwill

Clouds unloose showers.
Sunshine warms Earth,
Seeds spread flowers.
Nature feeds birth,

But.—Mortals unlease fury.
Their plans go awry.
Fate plays judge and jury
To all that live and die.

Like the moth and the burning light,
Man stumbles through the darkened night,
Forgetting lessons of civilizations lost,
Of Greed,—of Power,—of Human cost.

To wit,—The Babylonian,—The Persian,—and Roman rule,—
All built lasting structures—but—with the slavery tool.
Though adding great knowledge to Life's learning school,—
They all foundered for lack of The Golden Rule!

Peoples of the World—I beseech thee—Hearken!—
Unfurl your banners!—Hold Ideals high!
Use the power of the sun—'ere its' rays darken
And Life's rivers run dry!

(1996}

A Poet!—Why?

I like being a Poet—
Because I can freely write
What I think—
Then—file it away
To visit another day—
And—if proper—
Let stand my ink.

With tongue in cheek—
Poetry is—perhaps—
The rhythmic Voice
Of Life—our Egos seek!

(2004)

APPLES

Apples come in many colors—as seen—
Mostly pink, or red, or gold, or green.
Many orchards are commercially grown.
10,000 varieties are descriptively known.
There's the Cortiand, the McIntosh and the Golden Delicious.—
There's the Winesap, the Braeburn, and the red striped Grand Duchess.—
There's the firm tasty Stayman—for bridge players indeed.—
There's also the Baldwin—Musicians take heed!—

You can peel them, brew them, and make dumplings and pies.—
You can 'can' them, or dry them, or make puddings and fries.—
You can bake, or cake them, or ferment them for liquor—
Then mix with deserts for that extra fine kicker.—
You can glaze them to harden for chew—
Or use them for feed for life in the zoo.
You can jelly or chunk them or serve sliced in a dish.
They can even favor the teacher, if that is your wish.
You can jar, jam or juice them,—make butter for spread—
Or invent different uses.—They're endless 'tis said.
Moreover,—Why not emulate 'Johnny Appleseed'? Plant seeds to grow trees for
future need!
There even are rooters—for—Apple Computers! Now here's a fine
Note—from a Hobo—A Quote:
"The 'Big Apple—New York City—is My Home! I sleep in its' streets—in
its' alleys I roam. Now!—If I may, herewith, some wisdom toss—I
think the World—Is—Full of Applesauce!"

(1995)

A Sequel To A Famous Egg

Mrs. Dumpty, whose name lives in time,
Mothered The Egg in that famous old rhyme.
But—Hear Ye Kind Folks!—There's a rumor well spread
That all Humpty received was a bump on the head.
    To be more exact—here are the facts:

His coop really rested on the wall of a well
Into which a rolling Humpty awkwardly fell.
All the King's soldiers and all the Queen's girls
Couldn't find Humpty—more treasured than pearls.

When LO!—Deep in the well—swimming so free,
Splashing in water—as whole as can be—
They heard little Humpty's echoing cry—"I'm O.K.!
But I'm Floating!—I'm Floating!—I'm Floating Away!

They sounded the bugle and rang the big bell,
Then ran to the River that flowed 'neath the well.
There—on the bank—all muddied and mired,
Lay Dear Little Humpty—so tuckered and tired.

Friendly Duck Quackee knew what was best.
She bathed and then rolled him right into her nest.
She sheltered and warmed him—and neighbors all said
She even caressed him and feathered his bed.

Several weeks later—his shell cracked at last.
There stood spry Humpty!—He grew very fast!
Soon he was strutting 'neath his former well wall
Where, as Dear Little Humpty, he had his Great Fall.

So—Should you awaken to crowing some dawn,—
Could it be Dear 'Little' Humpty blowing his horn?
His—"COCK-A-DOODLE-DO!"—repeated again and again,
Is his refreshing—"GOOD MORNING!" and search for a hen.

(1995)

13

A Thanksgiving Day Dinner

Dinner time arrived. The kids were set for a treat.
The table was loaded with goodies to eat.
The Cook opened the kitchen stove door—
The Turkey—uncooked—leapt out with a roar.
It was Alive!—Untied!—Gobbling!—Distressed!
"I was Drunk!"—The sheepish Cook confessed.
The Turkey flew 'round the packed room.
It strutted through food piled high on the table—
Spreading its wings with a Bang and a Boom!
A window was opened and Tom Turkey flew free—
Heading straight for the backyard stable.
It was his Lucky Day—we all did agree.
The Cook—that was hired—was promptly fired!
The kids partied!—After nine they went out to dine.
Do you know what?—They didn't get thinner!
And—so ends the Story of that Thanksgiving Day Dinner—
The Cook-the Loser-and Tom Turkey—The Winner!

(2005)

A Visit To Our Capitol

Washington, D.C.
1990

I watched the peoples
Of our Country there—
Climb the long white steps
In the Sun's full glare.
The young and the old—
Children in groups—
In endless troops—
All eager—So bold.
What a sight to behold!
'Twas a joy to be near—to hear
Their laughter—their squeals
Midst the hustle and bustle
Of buses and wheels.

All compass points—
From near and far—
By air—by sea—
And railroad car—
They came
By cycle—by hack
I counted many
With baby pack.—
All colors—all creeds—
Enjoying the Liberties
Born of American seeds.

'Twas a Declaration—
Of the Moving Free
In this—
"Our Country 'Tis Of Thee!"

It needs to be told—
Of the pride in my heart—
To be favored to see

This heartbeat of peoples—
Each playing their part,—
Such Vitality—
In Our Capitol—
Washington, D.C.

(1990)

AWAKE!

The dials blazed RED—4:30 AM!!
The silent clock Screamed—SLEEP!—SLEEP!
My eyes Closed—and—Opened BUT an Instant later—
8:15 AM!—GET OUT OF BED!—SLEEPY HEAD!

Following the usuals—including the breakfast board—the newspaper's
Ceaseless ethnic and global war horrors—hurricanes—flooding waters—etc.—etc.,
I settled into the comfortable recliner,—a bit tired after the not-so daily walk.

My relaxing psyche was soon awhirl dreaming of last night's scary documentary—
"The Inconvenient Truth" about our on-going destruction of our Global
Environment!
Jeepers!—Has our Planet really gone off its rocker?!
Where is the Peace and Tranquility of yesteryear?
Is Nature sending us signals to mend our ways
BEFORE all Human life and its Civilization is destroyed?
My worrisome thoughts were percolating furiously!
NOW!—NOW!—We Must NOW soothe Nature's rebellious struggle
To regain its Life sustaining balance with a Sane Environment!

Peoples of the World—AWAKE!—BEFORE ALL IS LOST! CEASE
ALL HATRED!—EXTEND YOUR LOVE TO ALL!

The Globe was NOW trembling with powerful winds carrying endless clouds
Emptying oceans of water furiously washing away our drowning Civilization!—
WE DID NOT HEED ITS WARNINGS!!

SUDDENLY—I tossed and awoke in a sweat.———Is it TOO LATE?!

(2006)

A Window of Time

Silent winds fly thru space
Like the empty breath of Time.
Sun's rays slow a cooling naked Earth.
Bursts of lightening rekindle moments
Depicting scenes of the Homo sapiens past:
 Of War and Peace—Of Love and Hate—
 Of riches and song—Of unborn seed—
 Of Nature's blessings needlessly raped
 By unstopped witchery and greed—
All a vivid history of Life long gone.

And thus:
  Shapeless winds continue—
  As do endless tales—
  To unseen Souls—
  Driven by unseen Hand—
  In the Eternal Arena of Existence.

(2003)

Back Deck Agriculture

There's nothing like a tomato,—ripe off the stem.—
The stores charge:—a 'Million'—with hardly an Ahem.
So,—to counter economic pain, I invested in a plant for a dollar,
And earthed it in a bucket,—added a pole with a supportive collar.
With plant food and water, plus sunshine abounding,
Came little tomatoes, all sprouting in balance, surrounding
More yellow flowers that signal new growings. Such ever sweet
Yummies, hanging in bunches like grapes. What a treat!
So,—if you relish lazy farming,—
Without any back harming,—
Go!—Fill that bucket with dirt!
Insert the plant. It won't hurt!
Then,—watch the colors spread.
The yellows are first on the scene.
Then come the round reds,
All dangling in a background of green.
Pluck them!—Eat them—
Fresh from the stem.

(1999)

Beware! Here Comes Mr. Cold

The Common Cold is a vicious thing,
It rides on silent unseen wing—
And seeks out those who bravely say:
"Why take care?"—and go their way.

One day the weather turned inclement—
And Johnny had a sniffle.—
"Rubbers?—Heck!"—Away he went—
Muttering—"Piffle—Piffle".

Here is how it all began:—
There was Mr. Scheming Cold
Leaning on a corner can,—
When Johnny passed—Cold grabbed hold.

"Aha!"—said Cold—"You're just my man!"
Curses on rubbers and rules for health.
Those Doctors always plan and plan
More ways to ruin and steal my wealth.

What is my wealth?—you ask—
Hah!—Hah!—That, I gladly will explain.—
I find it a happy, loving task
To bring you troubles, aches and pain.

I find it quite a great delight
To see you cough and cry and sneeze.
I love to keep you up all night
With shakes and chills that make you freeze.

When you—KerChoo!—Kerchoo!—
And spill your burning tears—
I clap my hands and laugh at you—
And bring you bigger fears.

I always try to keep you ill—
To make you toss and squirm—

And when you think you've had your fill—
I just invite another germ.

That is how I operate—
And I have always found
Dumbnes is my best of bait.
I often win my round,

I nearly KO'd little John—
He almost was a has-been—
But he listened to his Mom—
And took his medicine.

Please don't think I always lose.
Read about Mr. Sniffle-face
In the Obituary News.
Here's another silent case:

Mr. Sniffle-bottom, with unbuttoned coat—
Marched out into the wind.—
It's a good thing his Will he wrote—
For today he's well coffined.

I engineered his headache—
And clogged his nostrils sore.—
He—"Pshawed!" me as a Fake.
So—Today he is no more.

Those germs Pneumonia and the Flu
Are pals of mine you know.—
Of all my friends they're just a few
Who follow where I go.

We germs deploy for action—
To search for those who say
That 'Care' is too old fashioned.—
On These we pounce for Prey.

I'll let you in on something
If you promise to keep still.—

We're mighty scared of schooling
And their medicines that kill.

Listen to My Sermon!—
I beg of you—Please Do!—
I know I'm just a Demon
That's always after You.

Don't listen to those Health Rules!
Forget my deathly ills!—
Don't wear Rubbers!—Be Fools
And I'll peddle you some chills.

And so—Dear Folks—is this Lesson told
Of the Common—Scheming—Fiendish Cold—
That right now is lurking near you—
With his friend—The Fiendish Flu.

So—Beware!—
Just be a Fool!—
Please Don't take Care!—
—CURSES on the Health Rule!

(1940)

Birds On The Wing

To flee the cold of frigid day—
Fair weather birds swarm Summer's way.
Like feathered clouds with whistling trills—
They nest the trees and window sills.

Welcome Summer Birds!—Welcome back!
All understand your instinctive track!

Next:—
      Winter Birds—by genetic mold,—
      Seek to challenge Nature's cold.
      They scare not of its' sleet and snow,—
      And frolic in its' frosty glow.
      When cold-cold winds begin to pain,
      They shelter deep in warm terrain.

And so:—
      With each new Spring, they build their nests—
      And birth their young to meet the tests
      Of Nature's drive to—Re-create—
      And thus—All Specie—Perpetuate!

(1996)

Born By Chance

(The Agony of Starvation)
(Two mothers-each holding their baby)
Healthy mother singing to her robust baby
Starving mother soothing her emaciated baby.

Hush-a-bye Baby—I'll rock you to sleep
    Cry Baby!—Cry!—Your skin is so cold.

A toy for you Baby,—a little white sheep.
    Out cursed Devil!—I don't want your gold!

Hush Baby!—Hush!—I'll sing you a song.
    Breathe Baby!—Breathe!—Open your eyes.

Four and twenty blackbirds baked in a pie—
    Your Mama is here,—I've chased all the flies.

And when the pie was opened, they all began to sing—
    Suck my finger Baby,—it can do you no wrong.

Four and twenty blackbirds baked in a pie—
    Lick the juice of this bug Baby,—it's better than dung.

My Dear Little Princess,—your hair is so fine.
    Just bare skin and bones—your black eyes shine.

Yes,—four and twenty blackbirds baked in a pie—
    I love you my Baby,—Please!—Please!—Don't Die!

Some day, my Baby,—you'll be in "Who's Who".
    You, my Baby, were born into Hell!—That's where we dwell.

My sweet little Angel,—Mother loves you.
    Move Baby!—Stir Baby!—I hear Death's Knell.

Rest your head on by breast.—Listen to the birdies sing.
    I have nothing more to give you,—My little Baby King.

Hmm—Hmm—Four and twenty blackbirds baked in a pie.
   Fly Baby!—Fly!—May your Spirit take wing.

(1999)

Broken

It flew into the wire
    It did—It did.
It flew into the wire—
    It did.—

It fell to the ground—
Made hardly a sound.
It fell to the ground—
    It did.

It lay there still—
'Neath the white window sill.
It lay there still—
    It did—It did.

Two long whistles—and three shorts—
    'Twas the CARDINAL song—
Twice done—loud and clear—
    So lusty—so strong!

    (Reader:—Please Note—)
    (Mimic the Cardinal Whistle Call here.)

Of broad beek—feathers red—
It nested overhead.—
    Now—it was dead!
    Now—it was dead!

Wrapped in green maple leaf—
I could still hear its' trill!—
    I buried it there—
    'Neath the white window sill.

(1982)

CLONING!—Way Out!

Today—there are many people moaning
About the possibilities of Cloning!

What if there were 1O Moses and 1OO commandments—or 10 Goliaths
Or inundating nudes painted by cloned artists like Andrew Wyeths?
Possibly several Adams and Eves in the Garden of Eden—
And—what if they didn't eat the apple?
How in the blazes would we now grapple—
Unclothed—with the frigid winters?—What then?

Should we cease all Cloning?
Scientists—and All—take heed!—Please advise!
Would the solution be a compromise?

Should we be moaning—
When we could have hundreds of Marilyn Monroes
And as many John Waynes or captivating Janes and Joes?
Or perhaps—say—a thousand Elizabeth Taylors
Cheered by cloned star starved handsome sailors
And others?—Ho!—Ho!—Ho!—What a show!

Maybe a hundred of me—
Or—a hundred of you?
Wouldn't that be quite a Who's Who?

This can continue without end.
And so—dear friends—I caution:—
Do not your body parts to Cloners lend!
I trust my imagination does not offend.

(1997)

COMPUTER!—HAVE MERCY!

Alas! and Alack!
Oh!—My aching back!
Sitting in the chair—
In front of the screen—
I'm getting nowhere!
Am I a 'has-been'?
COMPUTER!—I'm frantic!
I beg—show some restraint.
Don't be so pedantic!
An Einstein I ain't!

(1998)

Conscience

1994!
Will it be—of Peace—of War?
Wilt it be—of Love—of Play?
Will our horrors go away?
Will peoples learn to cope
Without gun—without dope
That burns all Life—
       That shreds all hope!

In fable—Wisemen often told
Our Conscience—is our Pot of Gold!
So—
Go—
Find It!
And Lo! =
   There—
      On a Golden Dish—
   Just as the tale is told—
     You shall behold—
       The Joys you wish!

(1994)

Corn Fields

Did you know that when your eye—
Quickly roams those fields of corn—
As you motor by,—
That some fields grew short stalks, and others high—
And you wondered—Why?
Well,—it wasn't the lack of rain, or irrigation
That caused the variation.
The field stalk heights were planned
By the farmer's hand.
The short stalked fields,—lessen rich soil waste—
And give bountiful ears for better taste—
To especially meet our consumption need.
Whereas,—the higher stalked fields
Give greater green yields—
To serve as nourishing animal feed.
The cows eat the husk, cob and ears.—All!—The whole thing!
But we,—we eat only the delicate ears for the joys they bring.

(1999)

Cups Of Cheer

The Fullness of Life is everywhere—
In the sea, on the ground, in the Cosmos of Space.
In your sleep's sub-conscious, in your wakefullness.
Give ear to the song of the waves!
Behold the dance of the leaves!
Let your senses pick plums for laughter,—of joys
That nourish the Soul.—They are all there!
Pace down!—Pause, for soon they vanish.
Make haste!—Now!—Taste the Fullness of Life
Ere its contents spill—unfiltered—and unused.

(1998)

Designed For Peace

From Ape to Homo sapiens—or,
    From Biblical Adam and Eve,—
After many civilizations—
    We cannot as yet conceive
An Eden for All peoples,
    Required for common need
To serve our lives with Trust,
    Instead of harmful greed.

We've conquered lofty mountains
    And traveled 'neath the sea.
We've even bridged the Moon
    And explored our Galaxy.
We've harnessed the mighty Atom
    And fly faster than Earth's sound.
We safely walk in distant space,—
    Yet Fiendish Wars abound!

Why not cleanse our thoughts of Evil—
And breathe Love into our Environment!

(1995)

Do It Now!

If we could harness treasured time—
And reverse its' spin to moments past—
Would we undo our plans long gone—
And venture from our lived-in cast?
Would we mend our ways of life?

And—if we can—
Would we respect our fellow-man?

It's never too late,—for the present flees—
And like its' shadow that follows fast—
It soon becomes the changeless past!

For,—even as you read this rhyme—
It's gone to rest in endless time.

So?—DO IT NOW!

(1990)

Don't Delay!—Enjoy Today!

More empty chairs!—More absent faces!
Oh how we miss their neighborly graces.
Those silent tolls approach ever so near.
The call is muffled—but the message is clear.—
Our numbers are dwindling as Time marches on.—
Come!—Let us fill full our cups with cheer
'Ere we're all Gone!

(1996)

DRUGS

Why do you break your body—
Amd drug your thinking cells—
And fill your healthy blood stream
With all those stinking hells?

A trifle tiny thumbful—
Can set your brain aflame—
And crumble all your balance—
Until you cry in shame.

Pass it by!—Just pass it by!—
And you shall surely see—
A pleasant Life and Future—
And a Happy Family!

(1996)

DRUGS!—YOUTH

Deep are the dregs of Dope!
Beware that stinking slime
That crushes Love and Hope—
And robs your Youth of time;
That smothers chance
In empty dance,—
Shamefully unending—
Socially offending—
In breaking—shaking fears
Through eyes that cry no tears!

Think hard Dear friend—Think Clear!
Project your sights one year!
A fling at moment's passion—
One scratch—or pill at play—
For exotic satisfaction—
Can rob real joy of day!
Pay heed this simple warning:—
You dare not go astray!
It's a challenge to your being!
Think hard!—Think deep!

Question:—
　　—Will your Future be of Mourning—
　　—Or,—of Mornings—bright and gay?

(1969)

Eligibility?

Was he handsome?—Was he rich?
Did he have the winning pitch?
Did he gaze into her eyes—
And whisper little lies?
Did he press her hand in his—
And stammer—"Gosh!—Gee whiz!"
Was he her steady Beau?
By now—you may have guessed—
She admittedly confessed—
That the Answer to All is—NO!
She married him on sight—
    Because—
        He,—could drive at night!

(1998)

Escape From Reality

Last night I dreamt of a Time and a Place—
That the Earth—torn from its axis—sped into space
And invisibly anchored—where Time stood still—
Where strange pulses recast Life to ever refill
Worn bodies with youth—and reshape all thought
Devoid of malice—and of all pain abort.
Was I an immortal reborn?
There I was—in a Dream so fulfilling!
Impossible!?—But my sub-conscious was willing
And trying to make sense, and so steer my Psyche—to make me feel
That, this journey through fantasy was Live,—and not unreal.
Though dreams stem from emotions and thoughts of the past,—
They are part of our Psyche—so illogically cast.
The uncontrolled dream lets the sub-conscious roam free
In the playground of Time—in all its Mystery,

(1996)

38

EXISTENCE

The Cosmos—
Our existing world,
Is forever framed
In Time and Space.

On Planet Earth,
Its seas spawned Life.
On land—greens flourished
And animals abounded.

Man came.
He hunted to live.

Man reasoned—
And civilizations flourished.

Man craved more—
And more—
But gave less.

Man faltered—
And fouled the Environment.

The Earth trembled—
And Man vanished.

The Earth—
Again lifeless,
Patrolled its orbit
'round the Sun.

In its Eternal vise
Of Time and Space,
The Cosmos—
A witness
To Man's folly—
Seemingly wept.

(2007)

FANTASY

Beyond the far horizon where the strongest eye is weak—
There lies Eternal City which since Adam we do seek.
I oft did wish to tour that place
By leaping through the distant space.
In shame I knew that mortal me
In yonder place could never be.

But,—'twas last night I slept a sleep
Whose memories I shall ever keep.
I felt a glow upon my head—
And—looking up, a strange voice said:
    "Follow me and you shall be
    Within the walls of Eternity!"

Amazed!—I glanced full 'round.
I naught could see,—nor hear a sound.
My eyes were closed as if in dream,
But,—Oh how real it all did seem.
My psyche—overwhelmed—never to forget—
I had wandered where Adam and Eve first met!

(1940)

Food For Thought

You wake up in the morning
Feeling rather fine.
You stretch your body 'round a bit—
Then table down to dine
Two tasty eggs with veggies—
With sausage on the plate.
Also,—an appetite to satiate—
Rates a bagel and some cheese.
And,—if you please—
Add a muffin and a roll—
Plus cups of wake-up coffee.
And you've reached your breakfast goal.
You dress and can hardly wait
To shop the market store
For groceries and meats—
Plus other foods galore.
This trip off repeats.

For lunch,—you down a sandwich,—
Plus an order of French fry—
With a salad on the side.
"I'll have that piece of apple pie—
—with ice cream!"—you decide.
Then,—the "More Coffee!" pitch.

In the afternoon there's shopping,—
Or loafing,—if you please.
Soon your dinner tune is humming—
And your appetite's in gear.
The telephone is ringing—you hear:
"Let's dinner out—My Dear"!
A drink or two with yummies
From the appetizing line,—
Then tasty filling entrees and more wine.
Ten add delights you almost missed
From the waiter's dessert list.
Finished?—No!—Not quite!

There's that little extra bite.
Now,—don't we look like dummies—
As we try to hide our tummies?

So,—Change your eating habits!
    Take a lesson from the rabbits,—
        Try chewing on some carrots!

Here's a tip—
    That you may follow:—
        "Eat ALL you want!
      BUT,—just DON'T swallow!"

(2001)

Four Wild Turkeys

Four wild turkeys resting in a tree—
One flew away—then there were three.
Gobble!—Gobble!—Gobble!—What a fine day!
Along came a hunter with his big gun—
Bang!—Bang!—Bang!—Then there were none!
Imagine his surprise?—They all flew away!

(1996)

Fractional Success

Wooley is a 'half-wit'
And fully fits the role.
He tried so hard to double it—
To make it into whole.
But,—he flunked his mathematics—
His fractions wouldn't fit.
They always seemed to add up
To the sum of 'Half-a-wit".

Soon came his able teacher
Who taught him how to pass.
His Diploma read—'Valedictorian'
Of the School's—'Un-graded Class'.

Then entered a Psychiatrist
Suggesting that he knit.
Today—his 'CRAZY' sweaters
Are labeled—"Made by A. Knit-Wit".

Now his toys are 'blocks' of money—
Has bankers counting it.
He's lauded as—"THE Business Man!"—
And he doesn't know the 'Half-of-it'!.

(1996)

Go West—Young Man!

Tho young—but of youthful zest—
He heralded the paper's suggestion:—
    Go West—Young Man!

Quickly—without hesitation—
He envisioned a glorious Conquest—
So he did!—He traveled fast 'cross our vast Nation.—

But,—when he reached Frisco,—Lo!—The Great Pacific
Brought forth a pounding urge,—Alas!—So Terrific
Was the beckoning sea—he could not resist The Conquest!—
With his zest for Life—he soon boarded a ship sailing West.

Onward!—Without altering compass direction—
The Lad would reach and settle down to new cultures—
Then again move on without change of election.
Always stopping to gather the history of peoples—he would find
Meaning to their philosophies and contribution to Mankind.
Thus imbued he traveled onward—but always further West—
And would settle down for long periods to study, learn and rest.

After many years—now Old and Gray—and wiser—he had
Persevered—only to Physically find himself—yet strong of heart—
Back to the Starting Point—EAST—from whence he did part
To "Go West—Young Man!"—as a curious lad.
A geographical twist indeed!

He learned that the Earth was truly round—
Replete with treasures and love to be found.
A youthful lark had become a Lifetime treat.
He had Full Circled the Globe—A Magellan feat!

(2005)

HATS!—HATS!—HATS!

Have you ever been to a department store
Where hats were racked in shapes galore?
Or, walked Manhattan's Fifth Avenue in the Easter Parade—
And gauwked at the hats that 'Les Belle Dames' wore?

From a global perspective, here's a short descriptive list
Of hats geographically worn that, in truth, still exist:
There's the Indian Turban, the Russian Sheepskin Cap,—
The Mexican Sombrero and the Bolivian Chullo with its ear warming flap,
The Scottish-Tam'OShanter and the unique Korean Fly Cage,
The Eskimo Parka-Hood and the Mantilla of Spanish rage,
The Indo-Chinese High Straw hat with its air space on top
To keep the head cooled while farming the crop,
The Raised Framework covered with Lace is a hat worn in Siam,
The famed Feathered Bonnet is the expression of the North American Indian.
The Chinese Headress, the Russian Chaplet, and the Yougoslavian Pill Box,
Add to these the hats of the seamen seen on the international docks.
There's the Derby, the Dutch Winged Cap and the saucy French Coif,
And the cocked sleek Straw Hat that sporty gentlemen doff.
There are Skull Caps of colors to meet religious belief,
Tribal Feathers and Quills for the Indian Chief.
There are hats made of wool, felt, fur, cloth and of helmet tested metals,
Also those made of leather, of leaves,—even of soft woven petals.
Hats geographical, historical, religious—that people have designed
To meet personal needs—or—their cultures to bind.

There are billions of heads in our vast global nest.—
Can you imagine the variations each thinks is the best?!

The aforementioned are but a few of the many. Indeed,—an infinite supply!
Descriptively endless!—Mind boggling!—I better now cease 'ere you cry!?

(1996)

He Sobered Up

It was a Nightmare!
Filled with 90 Proof—
He wobbled there.
His face paled—
Then flashed a silly grin—
As the floor came up—
And did him in!

When awake next morn—
His eyes red—
"It was quite a fling!—
Oh!—My woozy head!—
I remember not a thing!"

Then—slammed his head—
Not on The Floor—
But on the Pillow instead!

And vowed—"No More!"

(2005)

Higher (or Suspended) Education

She said—"I'll have a go
At Vassar when I become of age!"
Instead—she went for 'Go-Go'—
Suspended in a cage!
Pursued her course of yearning
For A Bachelor—to a degree—
And now she's gaily burning
Her Master's money tree!

(1969)

Home Action—World War II

A Declaration to your Nation re your Ration and Taxation,
    Really is the proper thing to do.
If you pay up all your taxes, you will battle-ax the Axis,
    And, in general, make the Enemy feel blue.

So dig deeper in your pockets, and you'll help flare up those rockets
    That will guide our boys to victory once more.
Buy an extra bond tomorrow; help your Government to borrow
    To insure the Freedoms Four we all adore.

Don't throw out your fat leftovers; don't discard your tin can covers;
    There's a salvage man collecting from your door.
Do not whisper to your neighbor, whether home or while at Labor,
    Concerning secrets or matters of the War.

Do not spend that excess money; buy those Bonds and make things sunny
    For the Future and the Peace we pray to come.
Get that Job to help the Effort, and you're bound to win the comfort
    When you'll see your Loved Ones marching home.

Surely People—You will answer to your Conscience and your Master
    That the aforementioned are the things to do.
So be faithful to your Nation, to your Friend and to Relation—
    And we'll Glory in our Flag—"Red, White and Blue"!

(1942)

Hoppy—The Frog

I am Hoppy—The Frog!
I sit upon a log.
You see,—
1 don't walk or run.
I jump—and jump!
It's so much fun!
Come!—Jump with me!
Gribbit!—Gribbit!

(2004)

I Am A Robot

I'm glad I'm a Robot!
I need not sleep!
I need not eat!
I have hands and feet
I can walk and talk.
I can perform surgery,
And detect perjury.

I must confess—
I need not dress!
Work time is limitless.
I seek neither pay nor pension—
Just intelligent invention.
I can build or destroy—
Even serve as a toy.
I can play music and sing.
If programmed—
I can do most anything.

I can be a tiny watch,
Recite an elegy,
Or be a mammoth submarine
—With atomic energy—
Powered to exterminate scores
In insane wars!
How I dread That Day!
But,——I can only Obey!
I'm a Robot!—I'm a Robot!

As a soldier-drone—Glory Be!—
If computerized—I can see
Targets to destroy,
Without fear—or joy.
Even be a Bomb—to explode
By contact—along some road.
I seek not victory or gain—
But an 'enemy'—Joe or Jane!
Goulish?—Hey!—I can only Obey!
I'm a Robot!—I'm a Robot!

I cannot Love or Hate.—
The Human controls my fate.
I have neither flesh nor bone—
I have no heart or pain—
Nothing to lose or gain.
I have no Life!—I'm a Machine!
I cannot smell the Green.
I'm a cog in The Cosmos Wheel
Cast as A Robot—without appeal.
I trust we are used solely for Good—
For Peace—For ALL Brotherhood!

Alas!—You see—
I'm designed to be—

A Lonely—Obeying—Robot!

I Wish I Were A Human!

(2006)

—IF—

If—guns were chocolate candy—
With bullets toasted wheat—
And canon thundered music—
Now—wouldn't that be sweet?

If the beat of boots were dances
And the Draft Board's door a gate
To gardens filled with flowers—
Now—wouldn't that be great?

If—wars were games of football—
And Generals umpire props—
With Nations cheering wildly—
Now—wouldn't that be tops?

If—the world was filled with children
Taught to love and sing and play—
And peoples' hearts beat kindness—
Now—That would be The Day!

Now—If—'IFs' made wishes real—
And chased away all fear—
We'd live in peace and comfort—
Hallelujah!—UTOPIA would be here!

(1994)

IF I COULD

If I could snap my fingers
    And bring those magic things—
I'd introduce a lion
    That warbles as it sings.
I'd invent a loony lady-bug
    That hiccups as it drinks—
And produce a scarlet owl
    That continuously winks.
I'd snap for dandelions
    To tame those buzzing bees—
And fill the moon with soda—
    And sip it as I please.
I'd paint the sky with cherries
    And pluck them one by one—
Then drain the clouds of water
    And squirt it at the sun.
I'd fill the world with candy
    And rain down chewing gum—
Then make all children happy
    By giving each a drum.
I'd change the ocean water
    To strawberry ice-cream—
And then—I'd snap my fingers—
    And wake up from this Dream.

(1984)

I Forgot His—or Her—Name

It was some time ago—
I met him at a dinner.
He was much thinner.
I forget his name.
It could be Joe?
But—I really don't know.

It's so vexing and perplexing!

Don't shed any tears!
It's only our aging gears!

Hence:
>Is it Tom, Dick, Harry or Jake?
>What difference does it make!?
>
>Fie—on the Memory game!
>We can't remember the name.
>So What!—
>We still know Him—or Her—just the same!

(1998)

I'll Know It's Over
WWII

When the burgles blare
    And the drums beat loud;—
When the peoples laugh
    And cry and crowd;—
When the fact'ries toot
    And the Church bells ring;—
When the Mothers and Wives
    Amd Children sing;—
When the hats go sailing
    Through the air,—
I'll know it's over—
    Over There!

(1944)

Introduction To A Poetry Reading

Hello Folks!—Here I am again
To torture you with thoughts and verse
Put to paper with pencil and pen
For good or better and, perhaps for worse.
I promise, I shall not insist
When snores and yawns persist.

(1997)

Katrina—The Hurricane of 2005

Katrina!—Katrina!—Lecherous Lady of the Sea—
You raped our fair land and drowned the Unlucky!
You danced with the Devil and showed no remorse—
Showering Death and Destruction with fury and force.

Have we wronged Mother Nature's balance for Life?
Do our treasures stir hatreds for wars and more strife?
Where is the Love in the hearts of all living?
There is so much Want!—Where are the Giving?

Peoples:—Are we too content?—Is there a message sent?
Need we change?—Need We Save Our Environment?

Alas!—Time speeds so fast!—Quickly—make Haste—
Lest our Seed inherit more Winds of Anguish and Waste!

(2005)

La Tete

We could begin,—with a dimpled chin—
But, we'll go instead,—to the top of The Head—
That shapes the Skull—that shields the Brain in its bony hull—
That sockets the Eye—for the vision tie.
Above,—the Eyebrow enhances winks and eyeball dances.
Protruding close,—is the shapely Nose—
Close by,—the Ear with which to hear.
Further south,—is the awesome Mouth—
With Tongue inside—as the chewing guide.
The delicate Lips—for kissing sips—
Surrounded by Cheeks and a dimpled Chin.
Within,—the Jawbone is rarely late
To flash its' Teeth with a winning grin.
Add—Common Sense—
Plus—a little Luck!
Put them all together.—
What do you get?—
You get—'A-HEAD'!
That's what you need—
To Succeed!
Enough said!

(1999)

Life

Life—like a top—
But spun from
The umbilical cord—
We wobble—
Then standing erect—
And tall—
Our spin grows weak—
And weaker still—
We lean—
And wobble—
And fall.

(1992)

Little Joe's—A BAGEL?

There was this lad named 'Little Joe'—
Who had a desire—especially to know—
How to make bagels.—His obsession grew.
Experimenting—he filled a pot with dough. ~ He knew
To spread it on a board.—But first he added water.
"WOW!" (he exclaimed)—"It looks like mortar!"
So he added some eggs, yeast, lemon and butter—
Plus—some sugar and salt—
And—stirred in a cup-full of malt.
"I'll let it rise a little"—you could hear him mutter.
He then kneaded.—Balled into 3 inch mounds—
He made two dozen inch flattened rounds.
Then scalded them with water boiling—
And brushed them with a fruity oiling.
Into the oven they went—to bake—
At 300 Degrees, or so,—he really didn't know.
After 30 minutes—imagine his surprise—
Each looked like a thick cookie cake!
But he was wise.—Very wise!
In the center of each—he punched a hole—
And named it—'The Joe—Joe Bagel-roll'.
The center 'cut' became 'Joe's Little Baguettes'—
Hailed as a Munchy Chew—also good for pets.
The public went wild—almost insane.—
They're flooding his stores from Frisco to Maine!
And,—What do you know?—
Little Joe—is rolling in 'Dough'!

PS: A Note from the poet:
    "Beware!—Tho the above recipe is copyrighted in rhyme,—
    It is purely imagined. Never made a bagel—I only eat them."

(2003)

London Bridge Is Falling Down

Remember—when as kids we'd sing—
London Bridge is falling down—
As we'd frolic, and dance, and clown
To the many joys the song would bring?

Now,—after long long years
    and aging gears
Another 'Bridge' has come our way
To once more let us fun and play.
It's "Duplicate"!—
    "The Modern Bridge of Sighs"!

At compass points we gird for battle—
North/South versus East/West.
Across square fields you can hear the rattle
Of folding chairs, of greeting cries,—
Of shuffling cards—for the Grand Contest.

Aides volunteer services a-la-carte.
Now—the able Director General's work is done.
With his—"Ready!—Aim!—START!"—
The Glorious Battle has begun.

The battle cry is—'Communicate'—
Take time to 'Evaluate'—
Then aim and bid, or pass, or double—
But,—whatever—'Stay out of Trouble"!

Swinging Clubs—blinded by Diamonds rare—
Attacked with Spades—fall to the trumping heart.
A humming babel fills the air
With team bidding often leaving
Exasperated partners stewing—
As their contracts fall apart.

The vanquished dolls and guys
Then cross 'The Bridge of Sighs'

When the grueling Battle is done—
Lo!—Cookies appear—glasses clink—
As warriors toast and drink
To the next Battle of fun.

(2000)

Lootie—The Friendly Lion

I'm Lootie—the friendly Lion.
The Forest is my reign.
I hum my snoring lullaby
To nesters in my mane.

I'm a victim of those frightful lies,—
Ask my friends the butterflies.
I carry all those perching birds,—
I never chase those scary herds.
I purr along with those buzzing bees,
And rub against those soothing trees,

I munch on fruits and roots and grass,—
And even wink at worms that pass.
No fish!—No meat!—Not even carrion!
I'm truly a freak—A Vegetarian!

See that hunter behind that tree!
Doesn't he know my philosophy?
He's ready to aim his gun at me—
And mount my skin in his library!

When Lo!—There I was in a public park.
My ears picked up a playful bark.
Mothers and children all around,
I heard their laughter—such magic sound!

They pulled my tail and stroked my mane.
An old man poked me with his cane.
I loved the world for trusting me.
I loved my jungle's mystery.
A squirrel licked my bulging paws.
I grinned and bowed to the crowd's applause.

When suddenly—a thunder clap
Awakened me from my mid-day nap.

I looked around.—'Twas all the same!
I was still the target of the hunting game!

It was only a dream!—It went so fast!
I hope the next will longer last!

So—Should you see me passing by,—
I beg,—Don't give me the Evil Eye!
See my Friendship List!—
Won't you please sign in?
For I'm only 'Lootie'—
    The Friendly Lion!

(1995)

Love Laughing

If you're a consumer—
    Of laughter and humor—
        You're on the road to good life.

But—if you find laughing—
    Is a thing that is baffling—
        You're in for unneeded strife.

Make light of perspective—
    Don't be too reflective—
        Sharpen that gleam in your eye.

Your tasks will be lighter—
    Your future much brighter—
        It's Easy!—Just give it a try!

(1995)

Lucy—The Ladybug

I'm that colored Ladybug
    That's shaped like half a pea—
Covered with many polka dots
    As you can plainly see.
My body—sheltered in shapely shell—
    But,—You could hardily ever tell
I'm soft inside with wings of lace,
    With little head and tiny face.
My six strong legs are quite agile
    To move with speed and thus fulfill
My search for insects edible.
    I clutch them with my mandible!

Transplanted by farmers to protect their trees—
    We feed on aphids and plant disease.
See my pretty lacy wings?
    I can stretch them out to fly.
But I stray not far from my fruit trees.
    Now you know the reason why!

So—If a wind should carry me afar
    And land me on your rug—
Please be kind and set me free—
    For I'm Lucy—your helpful Ladybug!

(1995)

Manhattan—in the 1920's

The present moves so very fast—
    And quickly speeds away—
But memories seem to longer last—
    Of our youthful yesterday.

Let us travel back from now to then—
    The 1920's—those changing years when:
Street lamps were lit by a man on wheel—
    Before the smog of the automobile—
When radio stations reigned supreme—
    And awesome television but a dream—
When ships crossed the Atlantic in fast five days—
    Before today's flights for overnight stays—

When children would walk to their neighborhood school—
    When the fountain pen was the fast writing tool—
When Ebbets Field was filled with cheering fans—
    When 'Coke' came bottled and milk in cooled cans—
When people traveled by train and by boat—
    When gallants sported the warm raccoon coat—
When the milkman's horse went clippity-clop—
    And you lived at home with your Mom and Pop—

When telephones were for the gabby rich—
    When Mothers had time to sew and stitch—
When you chewed on a stick of sweet sugar cane—
    And thirst was quenched with 'two-cents-plain'—
When corsets were part of the dress 'neath the gown—
    When the cop on the beat twirled his club up and down—
When toilets were flushed from a pull-chain box—
    When women sported mink and the silver fox—

When trolleys would clang as horses passed by—
    When ice-cream was big with hot apple pie—
You could ride a pony!—There were no X-rated smuts!
    When a penny bought Indian or red Spanish nuts—
Or delicious hot chick peas—with pepper at that—

Even tasty chestnuts from a coal fired vat—
When a pick would chop your sized piece of ice—
　　When tapes featured buttons of candy so nice—

When you winked with respect and tipped your straw hat—
　　When calories rated nil and you ate steaks and fat—
When chickens were flicked and all dressed by hand.
　　To many,—these are momentos of our Treasured Land—
To the old,—just fleeting thoughts of years long ago.
　　Were they the 'good ole days'?—We'd like to know!

Alas!—We now live in Time when changes are fast.—
　　If we don't move along—we'll be left in the Past!

(1996)

MATING

Tweet!—Tweet!—Tweet!
    The message is clear.
    "I would like to meet—
    A sweet feathered Dear!"

'Tis the mating urge—
    To meet and merge.

With a flap of wings—
    The Romantic sings
        His lusty breeding song—
Then rests his frame—
    In the 'waiting' game—
        For The One to come along.

In a well fashioned nest—
    They soon will rest—
        With seed to procreate.

Such is the thrill—
    Of Nature's Will—
        When lovers seek to mate.

(1994)

MIRROR!—MIRROR!

I stared into the Mirror.—What did I see?
A gray haired old body.—It was me!
I recalled those moments of years long ago
When the visions were different—decidedly so.

Oh Mirror!—Dear Mirror!—If you had memory and tongue—
Would you unreel my past?—Would it be wrong
To relive my reflections and volumes of thought
That as of this moment have all turned to naught?

When LO!—As though Magic had cast some weird spell,
The Mirror sparkled and it's dark shadows fell.—
Time spun back fast to those years when—
There I stood young and spry once again—
As though some mysterious camera lay hidden within
That recorded my reflections and thoughts that had been.

There I was!—Fresh in the fold!—
Oh!—What an awesome sight to behold!
The Mirror flashed faster with hardly a sound.
I saw myself growing—from a cell unwound!

I lay there bare—un-diapered—pure
Before the onslaught of social allure.
Soon crawling, then jumping—What fun!—What glee!
Mother smiling behind me—I must've been three.
Then—smartly in shorts—perched high on a stool—
Book firm in hand—quite ready for school.
Then followed the Teens—those glorious days
When love blossomed often—some Yeas—mostly Nays!

The Mirror still glistened.—More scenes did unfold
Of Memories long gone,—of stories untold,—
Of courtships,—of love,—of financial displeasure,—
Of sorrows,—of tears—and of moments we treasure,—
Of aches and of pains,—of laughter and squeals,—
Of plans gone awry and of ruptured ideals,—

Of children so playful—Such blessings
Of Life!—Those were the dressings!

Suddenly—The Reel ceased it's strange whirr!
The past soon became the same total blur!
Pray!?—Would The Magic Mirror more memories allow?
Nay!—It could not!—It's Time was right NOW!

(1993)

Musings

Poems are but candles of thought.
Some blaze like beacons of light—
Others flicker and turn to naught.

Earth is but a blackboard of history,
Of recorded civilizations long gone,
Erased by Time's endless mystery.
Ours too is but a tick in this Marathon!

Oh Mortal Man
Mix thy Mortar of Time
With the Past—
Sprinkle with the Present—
And—with these ingredients
Go build thy Future!

Kitten!—Dear Kitten!—How sweet your meow
Chasing dead leaves windswept 'neath the bough.
Soon you will grow.—A Bobcat you'll be
Hunting for Life in Nature's pantry.

(1997)

Night's Colander of Tales

Craning my neck far-far back—eyes blinking and dancing—
I envisioned a strange sight across the deep black sky—
A Colander—bursting with a zillion holes!—So entrancing!
A scene of lights—straining—from the dark on high.

Oh Colander!—Like a Crown of the Cosmos—
You un-sling Time's tales—showering fiery arrows
Midst Constellations—telling Myths of Ages that linger and grow—
Each in twinkling radiance—gifting all night—well past Sun's glow.

Such is the Sky—when Day's shade is drawn—
An Eternal mystery.—A Fantasy!—Wonders all
Evolving on Nature's black canvas.—How they enthrall!
Truly—All a Darkness of Awe—'ere the rays of Dawn!

Mortals!—Go!—Let your Psyche roam free!
Gaze to the Sky—and you will wonders see!

(2005)

OH MAMA—I REMEMBER

I remember MAMA—My MAMA—*I remember*
How you'd make me laugh and play—
How I'd thrill to hear you say
"Hush—My Baby Dear"
And brush away all fear.

How you'd kiss my burning eyes—
And soothed my anguished cries.
Yes Mama—I remember
How you'd wash and comb my hair.
You seemed to be just everywhere—
To blow my stuffy nose,
To button-up my clothes.

I remember Mama—Yes—I remember
That big round pail you bathed me in.
How you tweaked my nose to make me grin
And diapered me with a safety pin.
I remember
That long rough board you'd rub and rub
To scrub the clothes in that double tub.
Yes My Mama—I remember
How you'd rock and gently cover me—
And when my fevered brow gave fright—
How you'd watch and cradle me all night—

Yes—My Mama—I do remember
When I grew and saw the world
And my youthful plans unfurled—
How your presence made me feel
My lofty dreams were not unreal.

Oh Mama—I remember
How you fired the stove with wood and coal.
How you'd bake the bread and twist the roll.

Yes—My Mama
  "T'was a flavor of Life that's gone its way—
  Never to return—but for a moment today!

And now that I grow warn and weary,
When life oft seems so dull and dreary,
  I remember all those growing years
When you filled me with my childhood cheers.

Oh MAMA—Yes MAMA—I do remember
Your wishful sighs—
Your twinkling eyes—
  THANKS MAMA—THANKS MY MAMA
  FOR EVERYTHING!!

(1992)

One Summer's Day

The Sky was blue.—The Sun was hot.
What's to do?—The Beach?—or—Not?

I fixed a basket lunch—added bits to munch—
And fast was on my way to cool that Summer's Day.

The hypnotic hum of the ocean—
Its waves in constant motion—
Mesmerized my thoughts that Day.
I heard the rolling waves' chant:

> "We are the Surface of the Deep!
> Its Mysteries we keep!
> Listen to the Song of the Seas!
> Sleep!—and you will understand."

I quickly dozed—my eyes closed in trance.
When I awoke—my heart raced and pounded.
Sub-consciously, my psyche dreamt a dream within a dream.
It was about a long long voyage under the waves of the seas—
A journey full of awesome mysteries!
I could remember not one of them.

Awake,—the Sun was hot and searing.
All I could hear was the constant 'Chant' of the Waves:

> "We are the Surface of the Deep!
> Its Mysteries we keep!
> Listen to the Song of the Seas!"

What did I dream about?

It happened that way—
On that Summer's Day!

One Step More!
A Mother's Watch

Descending back stairs one fine Spring day—
A flapping of wings did warn to say:
"Take Heed!—My babies are in your way!"
I braked my momentum—and Lo!—
Just one more wooden step below,—
In an open nest of mud and straw,—
A warming sight—I seldom saw,—
There lay three eggs of royal blue—
Saved by a Mother's protective alarm.
She perched and watched from a nearby tree.
I moved the nest to cause no harm—
And placed it near a stairway post.
Did I upset the nest?—And thus engrossed—
I slowly backed away.—'Tis a story true!
There was Mother Robin—back with Family—
Giving shelter and warmth for wings to be.
How fickle is Life that a chance of step could play!
Generations were spared that fine Spring Day.

(1997)

On Youth

Youth!
    Go!—
        Explore
            Your
                Youthful
                    Pleasures
                        Today!

Yesterday is too late!

Tomorrow
    Will
        Take
            Your
                Youth
                    Away!

(1996)

Our Babel of Taxes

Whether National, State or Local,
One need not be a yokel
To know that a Society,
To obtain a sense of propriety,
Reguires a balanced brew
Of bases to extract its revenue.—
To meet its Government needs
It plants its revenue seeds
Of assorted taxes to meet the thrusts
Of the ever watchful Lobby trusts,
Later. Regs are spread on palatable dishes
Oft' to favor the Powers that be and their wishes.

TAXES!—TAXES!—TAXES!
Direct or Indirect.—Here's what we've got
In our perplexing tax melting pot
Covering individuals and corporations—
And other targe table configurations:

Workman's Comp. and Unemployment Insurance taxes on wages,
Social Security tax for the increasing numbers of old agers—
With foreseeable funding needs for the 'baby boomers',
Growing Sales and Use taxes on targeted consumers,
Taxes on incomes by source in various gradations—
Plus taxes on Personal Property and Real Estate evaluations.
There are taxes on Intangibles, on Franchises and Registration fees,
Special taxes on alcohol, tobacco and customs import duties,
Excise taxes on tires, tickets, communications, etc., as never before.
We also have, and justly so, Excess Profits taxes in times of war,
Gross Receipts taxes and Severance taxes on timber, minerals and oil,
Including taxes on food from the sea and on growth from the soil.
We have stamp taxes, tolls on bridges, roads and highways galore,
License fees on professionals, on gaming, traveling and myriads more,
And Alternative income taxes, Gift, Inheritance & Estate taxes not to ignore.
You need include County, Town and Villages, incorporated or not,—
All jostling and scheming and taxing to enhance their own lot.
Also tax shelters and havens and tax treaties abound in global trade

Letting billions of taxes slip thru the net—that never are paid.
To all, add the many nuisance and hidden taxes overlapping to a fault.
Alas!—The overheated tax pot is boiling—and there appears to be no halt!

The Politicians howl!—The Consumers cry "FOUL!"
TAX MORE!—TAX LESS!—All Parties scream—and fly high their rockets.
But,—no matter what—THEY'LL STILL PICK YOUR POCKETS!!

(1999)

Paintings In The Sky

Cottony clouds came drifting by.
I counted many in the pale blue sky:
A turtle, a goat with snow white hair,
An elephant, a dog—with upturned tail,
Both swallowed by a gigantic whale.
A fearsome gargoyle with jutting chin,—
Turned to mock with twisted grin.
Yes,—I even saw a teddy bear—
All afloat on invisible air.

And so the parade went on and on—
Truly an endless marathon.
So many metamorphoses—all changing shapes—
A gallery of treasures "midst misted drapes.

Lo!—I beheld Nature's canvas of brushless art—
Painting imaginations that stirred my heart.
'Twas as if The Circus had come to town—

And I,—I tagged along like The Happy Clown.

(2000)

Pappy's Tale

"Now look-a-heah Sons—I'll show ye how
I routed them Rustlers at Saw-kee-sow!"—
  His legs were bowed—his head hung low—
  He climbed the Oak and stubbed his toe.

  Now Pappy was hootching all that noon—
  "Take it easy Pappy or you're gonna swoon!"—

He hollered down:—
"Sons—do yah heah!?—
"I wuz a young-un"—"Had no feah!"—
"I cocked me guns and rifles foah"—
"Stayed up thet tree till my back wuz soah"—
"They came a-riden and a-yellin purty loud"—
"D'ya heah?—I figgers ten in thet Ruslin crowd".

"Bang!—Bang!—Bang!—They'z a-droppin like flies"—
"My guns were a-blazin!—I could see them's eyes"—
"The three that lived run like dey wuz wild"—
"Hot—Diggity—Damn!—Whoopee!—Whoopee!—
  Pappy whooped like a baby child.

  He was hanging like a monkey from a swaying limb—
  And he kept on whooping—there was no stopping him.

  Came dusk—he was climbing down that tree—
  It was getting dark and he couldn't see—
  He slipped and fell into a well—
  We fished him out and he sneezed like Hell.

  We dried him and wrapped him in blankets five—
  But when morning came he didn't make it alive.

  We prayed—then buried him in an oak box rough.
  Dear Pappy was licked by 'Old Whoopee Cough'!

(1996)

82

Plan Tomorrow

Tomorrow—
    Don't let it slip away!—
        Today—is fleeting.—
But—leap ahead—
    Into the future—
        And look back—
At tomorrow—
    For it will take—
        Its' place in history.
            So Go!—Make good use—
Of tomorrow—
    For it could—
        Some day be—
            The kindest—
                Measure of—
                    Your memory.

(1968)

Pleasures In Poetry

Wield the Torch of Poets!
    Let your spirits reign unbound!
Paint your inner passions
    That endlessly abound—
In ecstasies of wonders—
    Where Truth is ever found.
Peruse poetic pleasures—
    Whether free or rhyming verse.
Try those metered waters!
    Let your thoughts in search immerse!
Come!—Sail the mystic Cosmos!
    You'll discover hidden treasures
Within your psychic purse!

(1996)

POETRY IS BEAUTIFUL!

The Public cries out in dismay—
With emotions oft carried away:—
"What was that poem about?"—
Is the most singular shout.
With pedantic words like—'apodictic'—
Rhyming with—'eclectic' or 'elymic',—
A handy 'Webster' is really a must
To comprehend their hidden thrust.

Poetry should be available to enhance all instantly with warmth and feeling—
And not camouflaged with esoteric language that sends you reeling.
Poetry could then easily become a popular ingredient to our Melting Pot!
So—pick up your pencils!—You need not be a Milton or a Sir Walter Scott!

It's easy!—Keep vocabulary simple!—Just write!
You'll feel like a million—when you recite.

(2002)

Puppy Love

(Our family pet's letter)
(after being found)

Dear Judy:

When I was a little pup—
I remember—
How you used to pick me up
And pat my fears away.—
How you'd paper my bed
And see that I'm fed.

I remember—
Each was a beautiful day,—
I could tell by your tone
Whether I'd be getting a bone—
Or be chastised or scolded instead.
I learned right from wrong.
But,—I knew I belonged
When I curled up in my little bed.

I remember the day
When I strayed far away—
Forever lost in a world of fear.
When,—Lo! and Behold!—
I heard the happiest sound,—
The call of your voice coming near.
At Last!—I was found!
I remember—
I curled in your arm—
Away from all harm.—I remember!

So I beg: Don't think it odd
When I lick you and nod,—

Whilst adding a gleeful bark or two.
I'm only saying Thank You!—I Love You!

Sincerely,

WOOF! WOOF!
(Candi)

(1974)

Petunias

96 Degrees!
Blazed the meter nearby.
"Water!—Water!—We're so Dry!"—
Cried the drooping pink petunias—
Hanging from a high perched pail.
You could almost hear their silent wail:
"Water!—Water!—We're so Dry!"
Then,—with but one full kettle to the rescue—
Lo!—100 petunias raised their heads to sing—
"Thank you!—Thank you!—We love you!"—
Whilst a lonely butterfly—on the wing—
Happily danced from flower to flower—
Sipping the stores of Nature's power.
Yes!—96 Degrees!—It was a hot Summer's Day!
It's a true story!—It happened that way!

(2005)

Reminiscing!

Remember the days we challenged the cold,—
Its' wintry frosts when tales were told
Of sleds, of snow, of events more bold,—
Like skiing, or skating on lakes of ice;—
Of fires and drinks with rum and spice;—
Of party thrills. Yes,—we paid the price
Of sprains, of aches, of loves, of tears.

Those were the growing youthful years—
When a long—long future clothed all fears.
Today,—with that fountain of years drying fast,—
And tho those memories shall forever last,—
We should not dwell on the fading past.
We dare not let the Present stray!
Go!—Greet each shining newborn day—
—And—fill it full with Fun and Play!

(2001)

Restless Wings

'Twas a sight to see on a windy day—
A restless bird at work and play.
Perched high above on an old flag pole—
Dancing 'round and 'round again and again.
It would pause to rest,—then resume its role.
Strange?—
The whirling bird was a Weathervane!

(2002)

RETIREMENT

'Retirement'—is an Age-Old wish—
Serving bonus years on a Golden Dish.
We taste and gulp its' cherished food.
So free—unchained—indeed imbued—
We flex our unhinged—age worn wings
To roam new realm like Queens and Kings.
But oft'—too soon—we reach The Peak.
Our 'Top' wobbles. ~ Our thrust grows weak.
Hence—Take Heed Now!—Stand Up Tall!
Enjoy Today—Before—The Summoned Call!
Tempus Fugit!!

(1997)

RETURN?

Goodbye!—All Love!
I need 'Take Leave' now.
I'm beckoned Elsewhere.
But I shan't be far—
And shall return instantly
Upon your wish.
For—as you will it—
LO!—There shall I be!
And Only Then—
Can I return—
In Memory only—
To re-live fond thoughts.
There's no other way!

(1991)

Ripples

There, on wet canvas of the sleeping lake,
Nature's brush—invisible—painted
A likeness of itself;—
An ongoing reflection
Of the opposite shore.
Tiny fish dancing below
Lent an eerie tri-dimensional
Depth—in movement—.
All was so tranquil.
Suddenly,—expanding ripples
Framed and shattered its beauty.
The canvas had been pierced
By a pebble
Dropped from a disappearing bird.
Soon—ripples flattened.
The canvas—made whole again—
The painting reappeared,
Once more refashioned
In all its splendor.

(1998)

Robins In The Spring

I watched the Red-breast robins
    Hopping on the ground.
They picked and pecked and dug the soil
    And nary made a sound.

With beaks quite full they flew away
    And nested in a tree—
To fill the chirping mouths
    Of their feathered family.

(1995)

Roll Call

Ageless Time just rolls along
Singing its ageless welcome song.—
Without a beat—
Without a drum—
You feel its steady silent hum.
An ever changing marathon—
Of Those that were—
Of Those that be.—
And,—So it goes—
Just On and On—
With memories—
Of 'Those' Forever Gone.

(1997)

Sahara's Missing Trees

There was this little guy Max—
Who could swing his little sharp axe
The fastest in the camp.
He was the tree felling champ!

"Where did you learn to swing so fast?
You chopped that tree so quick!"
"Oh!—It's just a little desert trick
When I worked the Sahara Vast!"

"The Sahara!—
Are you kidding us?"—they cried—
"What trees?"—was the challenged roar.
Little Max—his head held high—replied:
"Not Now!—There ain't no more!"

(2006)

SENIOR CITIZENS!

TEMPUS FUGIT!

Where are the things that used to be?
Where are the things we used to see?
There once was a song—"Que sera—sera:
        "Whatever will be—will be."
Well,—many that were are no longer here!
Gone are family and friends,—even memories dear.
Our past stretches longer as our future shrinks fast.
So treasure all friendship for the moments that last.
    Take Heed!
Diminish all Ego!—Disdain Hate and Greed!
We are but flutters in Time,—Nature's gamble with seed!

(1995)

Shades of Noah and The Great Flood

(On Environmental Control)

Our golf courses are flooded., sewers run full—and that's not all.
The Lake Pontoosac dam lately measures more water fall.
Headlines scream: "Greenlands's Ice Cap melting faster!"—and more:
"They produce 50 billion tons of water a year"—as never before.
Air temperatures are increasing because of gasses since The Industrial Revolution.
We have a melting Permafrost with rising ocean levels. Add CO2 pollution.
Should an 'underwater sponge blowout' occur under the shoreline of the Atlantic Ocean,
Vast tidal and tsunami waves would inundate our coastline with catastrophic annihilation.

Terrified?—Who?—Me?
Scary?—Gosh!—Oh Gee!

Well Folks—get ready for the next Flood. The Deluge has already begun.
Lately we've been seeing more of clouds and less of sun.
The Media tells us that Global Warming is a fact and not a lark.
So,—get out your saws and hammers and start building your Ark.
Take along a few doves to test the settled waters, for you may perhaps dock
On far away Mt. Ararat or, if lucky, on neighboring high Mt. Greylock.
Also make room for all family and kin, including of course, your Mother-in-law.
Take along milk and cookies,—for there'll be no Stop and Shop replenishing store,—
Etcetera—Etcetera.

But,—really Folks,—all kidding aside,—
7,500 years ago Noah cried.
Today, The Great Flood is not a mythical lore.
Awaken!—All Peoples and Politicos—Take Heed!
Environmental Control is an urgent need!
Global Warming is not a theory anymore!

(2000)

Smile!—A Costless Donation To The Elders

Though blessed with Age—our need is Cheer—
As we look to the future for another year—
Or two—or more.—Is there a wishful limit?
There is no law!—just a Hope—to fulfill it.
Be it enjoyable—sociable—with Yeas and Nays—
Life wends its way through our chancing days!
So Peoples—Give the Aged a nod!—Let bells ring!
Donate a Smile!—All Hearts will Sing!
Try it!
Thank you!

(2005)

Snowflakes

Come!—Catch the falling snowflakes as they tumble down.
Loosened, twirling, spinning,—they glide on feathered sound.
Down—and down they dance to weave their blanket white,
Ever interlocking.—What a wondrous, scenic sight!
A million-trillion crystals—in cadence—fill the air,
Painting full the landscape—almost everywhere.
'Ere too soon they vanish—as if by strange command—
Obedient to the mystery of Nature's magic hand.

(1996)

Swinging In The Shade

Ho! Ho! Ho!—said the Jolly Big Tree—
Can you count the leaves that cover me?
I taught them to dance and taught them to sing—
I've nested all birds 'ere they could take wing.

There was Hootie the Owl—that kept all awake
Ever looking for field mice until after daybreak.
There was Squinty the Squirrel who always would stand
Whilst waving his tail as if leading a band,

I could tell you more stories
Of forest life glories—
Of the frolic and fun
'neath the moon and the sun.

Come closer Dear Children.—Don't be afraid!
You can play 'neath ray boughs in the cool of my shade.
You can swing from my limbs
Until the sun dims,
    Come back tomorrow!—Bring your friends too!
    I'll be here with my shade—just waiting for you.

(1997)

Sybil Ludington—A Female Paul Revere
Her Heroic Night Ride To Rouse The Minutemen
The Battle For Danbury—April 26, 1777
During The American Revolution

They came via sea—through Long Island Sound—
A flotilla of ships—Connecticut bound.—
Hustling and bustling with canon and gun—
The Redcoats' Command was:—"Destroy and Stun!"
Two thousand strong—under darkening skies—
Marched inland to attack the Town by surprise.
Their target—proud Danbury—its food stores and arms.
The British circled and struck hard on that Day—
In the Name of the King—for their Crown far away.
Soon—the Town was aflame!—The sky was aglow!—
Danbury recoiled from the Enemy's blow.

In nearby Bethel—only four miles away—
Col. Ludington was ordered to hold them at bay.
His militia scattered 'round far countryside,—
A horseman was needed to fearlessly ride
To rouse the Minutemen—to assemble that night—
To stop the Redcoats—to stand there and fight!
But—no Man was around to sound the alarm
To awaken the Militia from household and farm.

Now—Sybil—his daughter—the Pride of his eye—
The eldest of twelve—just sixteen of year—
Quickly stepped forward—"Father!"—"Why Can't I?"
"I can shoot and ride fast!"—"I volunteer
To rouse our brave men on all farms around!"
He knew her strong will!—Though not duty bound,—
He gave the Command:—"Assemble all here before dawn!"
Then added—"Beware of unfriendly Scouts that abound!"
He was so proud of Sybil—his very first born.

Sybil mounted her horse—reined only with rope—
And rode into the night armed with musket and hope.

Through mud and back trails—drenched by heavy cold rain—
For thirty-five miles—oft' clutching "Star's" mane—
She battered on doors and shouted her stirring Alarm:
"The British Are Burning Danbury!"—"Meet at Ludington's Farm!"

All through the night—so bravely she rode
To awaken all men—the young and the old.—
Body sore, blistered,—in sweat and in pain—.
She summoned the Militia—again and again.
She knew many farmers, their kin and their names—
Ever ringing the tocsin that hung by her side.
Onward—ever onward—she continued her ride—
Oft' at full gallop—oe'r mud field and hill—
Rearing and turning—she never stood still.

Midst the clatter of hoofs o'er bridges and stone—
The Message spread fast.—The Danger was known.
Soon shadowy figures—with musket in hand—
Assembled for Battle to protect their fair land,

—And thus—The Alarm spread through county and glen.
General Wooster, in Command,—counted seven hundred men.
Though greatly outnumbered—our Militia held ground—
Then forced the Redcoats to retreat to the Sound.

Historical markers in Pawling, Putnam, Patterson, Danbury and Carmel—
Record—'The Heroic Night Ride of Sybil'—the farm girl of Bethel.

(1994)

Thanksgiving Day

'Tis Turkey Day!—They say—They say—

    With all the 'trimmins' for it.

But:—

What do the turkeys say?

THEY SAY:

    "Thanksgiving Day?"—

    We can do without it!"

THE ANGST OF AGING

Slow down World!
You spin too fast!

You dry our years—
And dim our past.
Tho hard we try—
It ever seems—
You jam our keys
To doors of dreams—
And memories.

Pray,—Hear our cry!
Don't web our dimming sights
With global hate and ethnic frights!
Don't chase us from the Social Stage
To languish is some Waiting Cage!

Slow down World!
You spin too fast!

We've done our best.
It's time to rest.
Accept the sag
In our aging Flag!
Let it proudly sway—
'Ere it's laid away!

Slow down world
You spin too fast!

(2002)

THE ANTIQUE CHAIR

I'm a Chair!—I'm a Chair!—
A good old fashioned chair—
Now resting at the Country Fair.
I've traveled almost everywhere.

I've been sat on—stepped on—
    Kicked—even chewed,
I've stories to tell
    Of peoples well stewed.
I smelled them—held them—
    The short and the tall—
In hallways and bedrooms—
    Before they would fall.

Yes!—My back is still strong—
    My legs very straight—
Though my seat's a bit worn—
    I'm so proud to state—
That I still have my charms—
    But—like Venus de Milo—
I've lost both my arms.

Such is the tale—
    Of the old Antique Chair.
Take it—or leave it.—
    It happened!—I swear!

(1996)

THE 'BRIDGE' OF SIGHS

As Horatius is deemed to have said:
"I won't give up The Bridge!
I'm still alive and yet not dead!"
Tho his sword was broken—
His Heart had spoken.—
Was he dismayed?
Nay!—Thus,—quite unafraid—
He held high his Spade.
He Clubbed hard and fast.
His Bid for fame was unsurpassed.—
From North, South, East and West they came.
In their Bid for The Bridge Tiber by name.
The foe Doubled and re-Doubled,—
Despite all their Hands—'twas all in vain.
Our hero Trumped them again and again.
Horatius knew and tried every Trick.
He stood his ground and never did flick.
With his Gerber, Stayman and Blackwood,—
He Slammed them—both Grand and Small.
They shall not Pass!—They all understood—
As they bowed to the Winner who beat them all.
And thus does The Horatius Legend live in fame—
Like a Diamond in the rough—set firmly in stone—
So brave—so feerless—so all alone.
As we know,—"The Bridge of Sighs"—still stands—
Where visitors can repent their infamous Hands.
Where they can pray to better their luck and skills—
In The Game of Bridge—and all its thrills.

(2001)

The Charge Of The Golf Brigade

The Bull Horn blared The Order:—
"Ready your carts for Shot Gun Battle!"
What a moving sight we made—
All carts on Trail Parade!
You could hear our irons rattle.

With Egos quite enlarged—
Into The Valley of Golf we charged.
Were any dismayed?
Nay!—Quite unafraid—
We fired our shots that day
To the target far away.

100 Yards!—50 Yards!—10 Yards to The Pole—
Past hazards and bunkers to that little Round Hole.
Shots in front of us—
Shots behind us—
Volleyed and thundered—
Digging divots galore.
Sure,—we blundered!
We cussed and we fussed—
But,—Onward!—Ever Onward!—
This was War!!
In Truth,—let it be said—
That,—when Battle was done—
Friendships flourished again.

Wiser—older—but yet with yen
To vie in Golfs fulfilling den.

Hit that Ball!
That's All!

(2002)

The Cloud Burst

Like a nest full of restless hungry mouths—
    Cloud jostled cloud—each eager to swallow
The other—noiselessly and endlessly—
    As though guided by some enormous Force
In a shapeless wind—stuffing cloud into cloud—
    Until their binding turbulence expanded
Into one dark mass—pregnant and poised—
    Relentlessly pressuring its pulsating innards—
When suddenly—with a thunderous roar of freedom—
    It BURST from its confined captivity.

(1973)

The Copper Clown Statue

I'm a Clown! I'm a Clown jumping up and down
Animals and Acrobats!—The Circus is in town!
My face is white.—My hair is red.—
So colorful—from toe to head.
I'm sad and happy—half and half
I want to make you laugh and laugh.
See my act?—It's way up there
The tight-rope walk—high in the air.
I'm inching forward—juggling ball
If I miss one step—I'll surely fall
My balancing pole—just like a cane
Is the guiding staff of my royal reign
Only 40 feet—but far to go
To finish—Oh! Oh!—It's all my show!
If I tumble—please don't fret
For far below is my safety net.
So—Ha—ha—ha!—and—A Hee—hee—hee!
If I made you laugh—I shall happy be.

(1998)

110

THE CROW

While basking in the sun
One cool—crispy morn,—
Suddenly—a shattering Call!—

  CAW!—CAW!
  CAW!—CAW!

 What did it say?

It's steady tread and upright stance—
Turning and pecking as though in dance—
So full of Life—bellicose—so alert—
It strutted and cawed as if to assert:
  "I Am The King!—I have no Fear!"
  "This is My land!—Do you hear!?"

  CAW!—CAW!
  CAW!—CAW!

Amd—so I watched as he strutted away—
Crowing his Call on that fresh summer's day.

(1995)

The Ditched Cowboy

I shined my boots and combed my hair—
    And brought a wedding ring—
I thought I'd hear her say—"I Do!"—
    And hear the Choir sing.

I didn't know—she didn't know—
    My letter went astray—
She gave her hand to another man—
    I regret I went away.

She wed a handsome traveling man—
    So the people tell—
Then headed West in a wagon train—
    I wish they both do well.

If I could make the clock turn back—
    To that lonely prairie farm—
When I kissed her on that moonlit night—
    And sheltered her from harm.

Now there's nothing else for me to do—
    Except to ride away—
I shall forever remember her—
    Until my dying day.

So—Gidyup!—my riding friend—
    It's time for us to go—
We've got so many miles ahead—
    And trails we still don't know.

(1994)

The Dog and The Kitten

The Daddy dog—a Schnauzer—
    The Mommy Dog—a Poodle.
They had a little baby dog—
    We named her Little Schnoodle.
When Schnoodle was a puppy—
    She snoozed most of the day.
She looked like a Whiskered-Poodle—
    And quite frisky when at play.
She'd romp thru leaves in Autumn—
    Roll in grass in Spring—
Catch falling flakes in Winter—
    In Summer chase birds on wing.
Schnoodle was a playful dog
    With everyone she'd see.
She'd run and jump and bark—
    While racing 'round a tree.
On day—she found a kitten
    That somehow went astray.
When he kissed her sniffing nose—
    This is what she heard her say:
'I am lost and cold and hungry!
    And you're as happy as can be!'
'Woof! Woof!—I like you too!—Gee!
    Why not come into my warm house—
And you can live with me.'
    'Meow! Meow!—Yes! Yes!—Thank you!'
He purred—then scratched a flea—
    And off they went.—Their tails wagged high!
How playful they became!
    If different animals can friendly be—
Why can't people be the same?

(2001)

The Dumb Worm

Once there was a dumb worm.
He was about six inches long.
One day, just after a storm,
He wriggled his frame along.

He felt lost—
And thought he should have a mate.
And thus engrossed—
He wriggled on for bait.

Once more he stuck out his head—And looked around.
     "Oh!"—he exclaimed—
"Just two inches ahead
Is a cute little wriggling brown!"

He stopped—
He thought to thrill.
She stopped—
He thought—so still.
He wriggled anew—
She wriggled too.

But he was a dumb worm.
He was a very dumb worm!

"My Dear",—he whispered—
"My Sugar Plum!"—
The other worm let out a laugh
     And giggled—
          "Gee—but you're Dumb,—
          I'm your Other Half!"

(1944)

114

The Egg and The Bird

Today,—I am an Egg—
Ensconced within a Shell.
Have patience,—I beg—
I will hatch into a Bird!
Haven't you heard?—
Tomorrow,—
I'll produce another Egg!
What then?—
I'll hatch myself again!

(2004)

The Environment—An S.O.S. Dream

Take Heed People!—I really need SHOUT!
Tale Heed People!—I must move about!
All Life on the Planet is at stake!—'Tis Evil from Hell!
Take Heed People!—I've A Dream To Tell I

The World was aflame one misty morn—
As I collided with peoples—blank faced—forlorn—
Aimlessly wandering—all ages—many quite lame—
Each striving to Live midst a killing game
Of insane wars—all suffocating from gaseous CO2—
The deadly Greenhouse Effect!—The scientists knew
The Globe could wobble and that all Life could be expiring!
Was it too Late!—Was Man lax?—But Nature was trying
To alert peoples to thwart the Earth's apparent upheaval!
Doom's approach was relentless!—'Twas the Devil's Evil!

    Have—We the People—overstepped our Environmental Balance?
    Can we control our Fate?—Is there still a Chance?
    Take Heed!—All Peoples!—You are The Judge and Jury!
    Is My Dream but a Warning to beware of The Cosmos' Fury?

        Guilty?—or—Not Guilty?
           We Cannot Wait!
                WE MUST SAVE OUR ENVIRONMENT!!

(2007)

The Environmental Shadow

No More! An Omen

No more will acorns fall
Where the mighty oak once grew.
No more will leaves hang tall
Dancing in morning dew.

No more will roots bind together
Shifting grounds in devilish weather.
No more will Life be seen
Freely roaming forests green.

No more will Nature's vanes
Spin songs thru whistling trees.
No more will flowering lanes
Spread fragrance midst honey bees.

No more will birds abound
To nest a feathered brood.
No more will siblings sound
Their chirping cry for food.

The treasures of land, of sea and air
Exist for all to wisely share—
For Life—For Food—For Love—
For the soft blue sky above.

Beware!—Global Warming is at our Door
Spawning Hurricanes—deadly evermore.
Hearken!—Else, the Globe will Darken!

The Writing is on the Wall!
Take Heed—Peoples All!

Hear The Call!

Save Our Environment!

(2005)

The Falling Leaf

Gowned in Nature's brilliant hues
    As though brushed by magic hand,
Peoples flocked from miles around
    To drink the colors of the land.

Alas!—I, but a single leaf,
    Once alive and green,—
Now dried by draught and
    Autumn wind,—am seen
In shriveled form as I twist
    And tumble to the ground—
Detached, alone, forlorn—
    Downward—downward bound,—
Part of an endless wave
    To a waiting surface grave.

Do you remember my shapely form
    When I swept the smells
        And cleansed the air—
Sheltering feathered flock—whilst
    Artists' paints would canvas me—
        As I danced and posed up there?

Hark!—My Mother-Father Tree,
    Once cloaked with sibling green,
        Soon will winter naked be.—
But,—they stand so Straight and Tall!
    Though I leave Today,—Tomorrow
        They will birth their young,—
            Again to heed their Rooted Call!

Cosmic Forces do chance Life!
    The Plant Kingdom was cast for me.
'Tis better to have so Lived—
        Than not at all to Be!

Such is Nature's endless rhyme
Of Cycling All in Ceaseless Time!

(1995)

The Fullness of Life

Take Heed!
We are but chance of seed,—
A silent Tick in endless Time—
Dressed in Mortal Cloak.
Make haste!—Relent!
Enjoy Life's senses now!—Find
The pleasures they evoke,—
'Ere the Tock is spent
And all past is left behind.

(1998)

The Hole In One?

Well,—sure as shootin'
The fans were rootin'
When they saw the ball in the air.
It hit the flag pole—
And dropped into the hole—
But,—Alas!—It disappeared.—Where!?

Well,—you see,—a crafty old mole
Spotted that Green with the hole—
And burrowed beneath its tin wall.
When he heard that dull click—
He did his Mole trick—
And scurried away with the ball.

(2002)

The Ice Cube Tree

"Wouldn't it be nice"—
Said Little Johnny—
As he planted
A cube of ice
In the ground.
"It could grow
Into a tree!"

When—Lo!—
As if from Magic seed—
With a WHOOSHING sound—
It BURST from the ground.
It grew—and—GREW—
Spouting
Frozen leaves of green.

Such Beauty
Had never been seen!
Dangling fruits of ice—
Glittering in many colors—
Were dancing—
And tinkling
A cool refreshing tune!

All—under a hot midday Sun!

Suddenly—a bee buzzed by!

Johnny awoke!

    There!—On the garden floor—
      Lay a puddle of water!
          It's origin—A Mystery?

(2004)

THE LAMENT OF THE HOBO

MISTER!—Please don't look away!
Please listen to what I have to say!
I'm a Hobo!—I'm a Hobo!
That sleeps in the City's dirty streets.
I'm a Hobo!—I'm a Hobo!
Never know when I'll get my eats.

It all began with financial debts
That led to drink and gambling bets.
I'd sell my shoes for a bottle of booze.
I'd never win!—I'd always lose!

I'm a Hobo!—I'm a Hobo!
Never broke the law!—Just lost my will!
Lost my soul for a dollar bill!

I'm a Hobo!—I'm a hobo
With a beaten face and a dead blank stare.
Kicked around just everywhere!

MISTER!—PLEASE!—DON'T walk away!
MISTER!—LISTEN to what I have to say!

—HEY!—HEY!—???—.

(1994)

The Live Pebble

I spied a pebble 'neath a tree—
Of pinkish-white—such symmetry!
I stooped—But ere I touched its form—
Behold!—An Egg!—A Life 'unborn'!
There it lay.—So pure!—So clean!—
A fallen gem upon the green.
Carried in my warming palm—
I sheltered it from further harm.

I wove a home of leaves and grass—
A fruitless gesture!—and—Alas!—
So gently—so as not to crush—
I tied it to a 'Bottle Brush'.

Covered with straw,—a blanket light—
To give it warmth from chill of night.
There it rests on a branch up high—
Nestled 'neath the blue-gray sky.

Fate decreed its fatal blow—
And so this Life will surely go.
If it could hatch—and had it grown—
'Twould sow its seed and surely flown
Among the trees—and built its' nest—
And be the Hunter in the survival test.

But—Such is Nature's ceaseless clock—
It Gives—then Takes—with tick and tock!

And so it happened on that sunny day!
I did my best—then walked away.

Post Script:
>   We are all Seeds of Chance—
>   Buffeted by Winds of Fate!

The Lone Coyote

I'm the Lone Coyote from the wild-wild West.
When the moon is high—I howl the best.
My fur is soft—a yellowish-gray.
I wake at night and rest by day.

Once a prairie wolf that roamed so free—
I preyed mostly on pests like the rat family.
Rarely did I hunt stock—even when they'd stray—
Tho I was oft target for Hunters' play.

Alas!—One Day I was trapped—and caged.
Thus confined—I slowly aged.
Even so,—I was proud!—With head held high—
I talked to my pack 'neath the moon-lit sky.

But Hear Ye All!—Now mounted for all to see—
'Tis I—The Lone Coyote—sculpted from Tree—
To ever howl in the dark of the moon lit park.

I beg!—Listen carefully!—Think of me!

I'm no longer hunted!—There is no fear!
With imagination—you will surely hear
My eerie call and dog-like bark.

My Spirit is back in The Woods!—

I'm FREE!—I'm FREE!

Post Script:
    Except perhaps—for Woodsy The Woodpecker—who's taken a fancy to me.

(2006)

The Marathon

There are no markings on this Silent Clock—
It's Father Time!—And as his presence nears—
Ever closer—there are no tears.
The Chosen cannot countermand
His shrouded face and outstretched hand.
The air lies still.—The round is square!
His ceaseless gait—gathering Flock—
A Lifeless Chain from Everywhere!
The Eternal Marathon!

(1997)

The Mighty Oak

I am
But a piece of wood
Born of tree—
First born of seed—
An acorn.
I remember
Clutching for life,—
Bouncing naked,—
Rolling—
Soon imbedded
In muddied ground—
My womb—
My shelter.
Nourished,—
I rooted.
My Fate to be
A sturdy Oak!

One Day—Ahoy!
Axes and saws
Hummed and
Shaped my innards.
I gallantly
Sailed to Sea!
Time aged me.
A Devil Storm
Raged me
And broke me.
Now—
I am but
A piece of Oak—
Torn—
Alone adrift—
Flotsam—
In an Angry sea.

Please
Save me!
Take me!
Mold me!
Mount me—
For all to see—
The memory
Of
A Mighty Tree!

(2007)

The Missed Signal

Paul Revere leapt on his horse—
    And rode he thought so well.
He clutched his hat and clamped his spurs,—
    The horse sped on its way.
"The British Are Coming—The British Are Coming!"
    He knew his lines to tell.
But,—when his foot slipped the stirrup,—
    Things were not O.K.!

Back on his horse—he tried again.—
His leg was bruised and gashed.
When the horse braked at the bridge,
Into the lake he splashed.
Enough!—he said.—It's not my day!
And went back to his farm.
He changed the course of history!
He cancelled the Alarm!

So now there is no baseball,—
No Vegas gambling Hall,—
No hockey sticks,—no cowboy tricks,—
There is no baseball,—
No franks and beans,—no greasy grits,—
No good old cherry pie,—
No Congress wars,—no lobster claws,—
No ham-n-eggs on rye!

We're Subjects of the Royal Queen—
With fish and chips each day!—
Brittania still rules the seas!
There is no U.S.A.!!

(1991)

THE MOON

Now full of face—you look so pale!
May we be privy to your tale?
Tell us of the things you see—
Of the Agony and the Ecstasy
On Mother Earth.—Its Mirth—Its Fears—
You've been its Satellite for all its years—
Of its aging process—of its Wars and Peace—
Repeating cycles that never cease.
You are The Watchdog of Global change!
Pray tell!—Will you a Witness be—
Before The Judge of Eternity?

(1996)

The Old Golf Ball

(Sung to the tune of "I'm An Old Cow Hand")

I'm an old golf ball,—
That's been around.
I've been Mulligan'd,
And bushes bound.
I've missed my greens,
And I've missed my putts.
I've been scarred and maimed
With brutal cuts.
My ego's low,—but worst of all,—
I'll soon be gone.—I'm the Water ball!

(1998)

The Old Man and His Rock

In fair Lenox, Mass.—on New Lenox Road—
Go East of Route 7,—nigh 1/4 mile.
You will—on the right—surprisingly see,
Just off the curb—nestled so free—
An Enchanting Rock!
It is The Old Man's Rock—
That Nature,—in its mysterious way,
Shaped into an inverted bowl
Like some rounded stage,—
Structured in an eonic age,—
Now visibly risen from the ground.
It is fully topped with simmering moss
That lends a colorful and spelling gloss.

Should you linger a while,—
You may see the Old Man.
Oh,—what a friendly smile!
He lavishly encircled its girth
With fine gardening—to give birth
To bursting flowers and green.
What a sight to be seen!
It dazzles the eye
Of all passers-by.

The Rock,—and strangely so.
Appears to radiate a presence
Of serenity,—and of well being
For continuing sub-conscious healing.

Pray,—Dear Rock—
Please do tell—
Where is The Old Man?
I've been away
For many a day.
You look a bit wan.
I trust he is well!

(1999)

The Old Man and The Shadow

There he was—a wierd Old Man—
Jumping—hopping—down the street—
Whirling—turning—bending—
But—always looking at his feet.

"Excuse me Mister!"—I politely asked—
"What is your act?" He answered:—
  "This is no game!"—(his face red)—
  "Kind Sir—
  I'm perplexed!—Do you know
  How I can step on my shadow?"
    (that then was just a step ahead)

I smiled and answered:
  "Rest now—tired man!—
  You will—and very soon!—
  You will step on it—At Noon!"

(1996)

The Old Old Clock

I'm now and old and worthless clock
    That used to tick and tock all day—
And when the people passed me by.
    This is what I'd hear them say:

It's time to rise!—It's time to eat!
    It's time to feed the sow!
It's time to cut and bale the wheat!
    It's time to milk the cow!

And so—I went for endless years.
    I'd tick and tock my aching gears,—
        And as I'd age
        In my old cage—
I'd hear the same old chant—
But,—with a modern slant:

It's time to jog!—It's time to call!
    It's time to meet the train!
It's time to watch the T.V. show!
    It's time to catch that plane!
It's time to set that V.C.R.!
    It's time to computerize!
It's time I made that hole in par!
    It's time to exercise!

For years I ticked and tocked with fright
My wheels were worn. My gears were tight.
I dreaded That Moment—The Time of Sleep
When my innards would find some rubbish heap!

But Fate was kind I must confide.
My body has been Mummified!

Now, standing Tall
Sans tick or tock,—

I'm The Antique Clock
In The City Hall!

(1995)

THE PAIL OF RED PAINT

LO!—I give you this Pail of Red Paint—
    A Brush—and the Canvas of Time.
What will you depict?—

    The red glow of Life?
Or—
    The drippings of Death?

      Now!—Go Paint!

    History will be the Judge.

(1984)

The Party On The Hill
With Jack and Jill

Jack and Jill went up The Hill
With a pail of ice-creamed flowers.
It was a party for their childhood friends
That echoed for many hours.

There was Jack Horner—in the corner—
Eating his pumpkin pie.
Standing nearby was Little Bo Peep
With her snow white sheep—
You could hear their Baa Baa cry.
Little Miss Muffet—with her tuffet—
Was eyeing the Spider nearby.
Romping around—meowing in sound—
Were the three little kittens—
Who had found their mittens.
Humpty Dumpty was sitting on the wall.
He didn't make a sound until His Great Fall.
Holding hands were Red Riding Hood and Goldie Locks
Laughing at The Big Bad Wolf wearing GranMa's socks.
Even The Three Bears were amused—
Tho they looked a bit confused.
Elsie The Cow was chewing her cud
Whilst The 3 Little Pigs were rolling in mud.
There were many dancing on the floor.
It was like a Country Fair—but more!

When the ice cream pail rang—EMPTY!—
Jack and Jill would run down The Hill—
And—Lo!—Their was Mother Goose—
Smiling—Ready with a pail refill.
She loved all at The Party.
They had met so many times—
And starred in all her stories—
And shared her fabled rhymes.

Thanks!—Dear Jack and Jill!
Thanks for The Party on The Hill!

(2005)

The Pendulum of Time

Ageless Time!—
    The Eternal Clock!—
        Your Pendulum swings—
           In endless grace—
               In steady pace.—
                  You Tick and Tock
                    All Time away!

You have no beginning—
    You have no end—
        One cannot transcend
           The forbidden Secret
               Of your ceaseless measure.

Alas!—We are—
    But a breath in Time—
        Mortals suspended—
           Like puppet toys—
               In Life's unstable rhyme—
                  Seeking gasps of pleasure,

(1996)

THE POET'S RECITAL

The seats were filled—10 rows deep.
Silence reigned,—not even a beep.
The Poet stopped—and raised his eyes.
Imagine his surprise!?—
The Audience,—was fast asleep!!

(1999)

The Pot of Gold

Who are you—Old Man?
    They queried his presence there—
    In Royal Robe with piercing eyes.

"Call me—'Time of Everywhere'!"

"Pray tell—we wish you well,—
    What does thy presence here?"

"To quell thy thirst in your search
    To find The Pot of Gold!"

"Do you know the secret—Old Man
    Of the path to Treasure's Place?"

"The Place is here and everywhere
    Where breath of Life exists!—
    The Pot of Gold is Life that's born
    From your Mother's womb,—
    And exists only until Death's due.
    So cease your search and live your Life,—
    Your Pot of Gold is You!"

(1995)

THE PULSE OF THE POETS

LO!—Feel the pulse of the Poets!
    They are a special kind.—
They ideate in musings
    Where you will treasures find.—
Just as bees bring Life to flowers—
    Poets pollinate the heart
To soothe the searching Psyche
    In our Cosmos changing Mart.

(1996)

THE RATTLE HYMN OF THE REPUBLIC

1992

The canon roared—
Missiles soared—
To whip destruction in the sands.
DEATH stretched up with stiffened hands—
Lifeless—Reaching—All ignored!
From shot and shell—so many fell.
The Devil had loaned that place to Hell!

That was The Desert War!

Now—we hear the rattle
Of other woes.—Who knows
What the future will be!

"Oh Say Can You See?"

(1992)

The Return Of Robin Redbreast

Welcome Back!—Red Robin—
    How spirited you dance—
Bending—standing—hopping—
    Searching for romance—
Or—better still—hoping
    To build a home perchance?
Did you winter in the South
    When you fled the North cold air
That covered trees so bare?
    Where are your young of last year
That crowded your stuffy nest?
    There were three—I can verily attest!
Welcome Back!—Red Robin—
    It's so good to have you here!

(2005)

THE SMOKING ROMANCE

He was ninety—She was too—
When they vowed—"I Do!"—"I Do!"
She fed him and blessed him—
And even caressed him.
She catered his whim and his cue.
But,—when he puffed his cigar—
He went just too far!—
"It's either me or the smoking!"
He thought she was joking—
And lit up his stinker in bed.
She blessed him and dressed him—
She even caressed him—
Then shot him right thru the head,

(1990)

The Snow Man

We packed a ball of sticking snow—
    Rolled and rolled—we made it grow—
Then shaped and built a body tall—
    From a teeny-weeny white snow ball.

We placed a hat upon his head—
    And added tinsel of color red—
To give him eyes—a nose—and lips—
    Then twigged a belt above his hips.

A muffler 'round his sturdy neck—
    Just below his shapely chin—
Then Eric yelled his name by heck:—
      "It's Frosty!"
    And Frosty answered with a grin.

(1987)

The Talking Golf Ball

I'm just a dimpled golf ball—
But,—I can see and talk.
My game can be delightful
Or be so very frightful
If you scare and tend to balk.

Now—Here's the player of extra girth
Whose awkward stance fills one with mirth.
His trouble is—stooping to the ground.
When he bends—he tries to tee me.
"Mulligan!"—he cries.—"A Free-B!"
Though he may be a social climber,—
Perhaps a poetic rhymer,—
But,—to golfers he's a duffer so unsound.
Methinks I'll give him a scare.
Perhaps raise his balding hair.
"Hey—Mister!—Quit your squawking!
Yes—It's me—your Golf Ball talking!"
His eyeballs roll.—His eyelids flutter.
"A talking golf ball?!"—I hear him mutter.
"It can't be!—It's staring at my eye!
I should have skipped that extra rye!"

By now Fat Man is all acquiver.—
His frame begins to shiver.
"Mister!—Just keep your head down lower.
Swing your club a little slower.
Spread your feet a little wider.
Slow down!—You're not a jockey rider!
Listen!—Keep your eye on my center dimple!
Bring your head down!—Now that's simple.
Now swing!—Bend your knee and turn.
WOW!—You hit me!—Watch me burn!"
I traveled far for quite a while.
"Attaboy Fatman!—Let's see a smile!"
I sailed so far—and—Oh,—So high,
I disappeared into the sky.

His friends—aghast—were truly jarred.
They stared—and stared—and stared so hard.
And Fatman,—he laid down his club.—He Quit!
He didn't believe that record hit.
He started to stutter.—
He was heard to mutter,—
"A Talking Golf Ball?!
I'm Nuts!—That's All!"

So—If your handicap is growing,—
And you're feeling kinda blue,—
Just find a talking golf ball—
And it will tell you what to do.

(1994)

The Tiny Ant's Discovery

I'm just a tiny crawling ant
    That climbed up on a tree.
I climbed so high and reached the top,
    And I could clearly see
The stars, the moon and evening sun
    All hanging in the sky.
I saw strange birds with steel gray wings
    And a lonely butterfly.

There is a world above the ground—
    So big—so wide—so free!
I held my breath and gripped my twig
    In utter ecstasy.
When along came a whirling wind—
    I flew just like a bee
And landed on a swaying leaf—
    So soft and tenderly.

I told my little crawling friends
    Of the wonders of the world.
They were eager to discover more
    And soon their flags unfurled!
We formed a moving little band
    And crept upward from our mound
To investigate the outer world
    From our homes built underground.

(1995)

The Turtle's Dream

Give me scales—I'd be a fish
And swim so fast and far.
With jets for wings, I'd make a wish
And chase a shooting star.

I'd climb the fabled bean stalk
And float on clouds so soft.
I'd skip and jump and even hop
And if I could, I'd talk.

I'd buzz the buzzing bumble bee.
I'd even catch a fly.
I'd kiss a praying mantis
And then I'd wonder why.

I'd shed my bony anchor
And dance around skin bare.
I'd do a double somersault
And race that silly hare.

But—Alas!—I must be dreaming—
I can barely move around.
I'm locked—forever crawling—
I'm a turtle on the ground!

(1973)

The Watch

Said the cat to the rat—
You're getting too fat,
I'm gonna get you for that.

Said the rat to the cat—
You're a stupid fat cat,
I'm not a rat—I'm a bat—
And you're not gonna get me for that.

And with that—the sly old bat
Bit the cat—the fat old cat,
Then flew atop a hanging hat,
And laughed and laughed at that.

He's a sly old rat—with wings at that
Said the cat—the fat old cat—
I'll get him for this and that.

And so they sat—the cat and the bat
Watching each other grow old and fat—
And—That's That!

(1957)

"The Watch"—A Sequel

(About The Cat and The Bat)
45+ Years Later

One day—along came The Poet
With pencil and pad.
Saw The Cat and The Bat—
Both old and so sad.
Feeling sorry for the two—
He knew just what to do.
After all,—he had set the stage.
So,—with poetic license—he'd add a page.

"Stop all this nonsense!"—he wrote on the pad.
"There's no rhyme or reason to be so mad!"
He scoured back alleys and yards for miles around—
Visiting belfries—and caves—that rose from the ground.
He hung posters and greetings for all friends to see—
"COME TO A CAT & BAT PARTY—for a HAPPY FREE-BE!"

He fed them meat bites with mosquitoes for filling.
'Twas a friendly 'Blast'—uniquely quite thrilling.
They meowed and flapped wings—all sang together.
It was truly Great—and so was the weather.
They cavorted all night—to the wee hours of morn—
Greeting the new Day at the break of Dawn.
You could hear the Old Cat and Old Bat rolling in laughter—
—Even hugging and dancing.—Sure!—They lived happily ever after.

Believe it—or Not! It really happened!
—In a Dream that was penned—
Into this tale by their Poet and Friend.
          —The End—

(2003)

The Wheel Of Time

Come,—fleeting thought!
Let us spin The Wheel of Time!
Forward—or—Back?
Tis all the same!
Birth—and—Death!
Love—and—Hate!
War—and—Peace!
Good—and—Bad!
Like drum beats—
That repeat and repeat
The Peoples' history,—
All an enigmatic mystery—
In The Wheel of Time.
Is it Nature's ceaseless ploy
To first Create and then Destroy?

(1968)

The White Birch Leaves

Once bone white,—my leaves would dance
On limbs stretched high to enhance
The bird—the squirrel—and the painter's eye.
"Rest 'neath The Birch for shade!"—(a Summer's cry).
I even thrilled to carvings of the lover's lie—
And to all tattoos—now rottings of memories gone
In Life's enchanting marathon.
Alas I—I stand alone!—I've shed my bark,—
Gone is my green.—The sun is dark.
My roots are dry.—My branches hang
Grotesquely bare.—My leaves once sang
Such joyous sound.
Now,—the clutching wind blows thru
My weakened frame—
Listen to its haunting chant!:—
"Dust unto dust!—
You have a rendezvous!—
Recycle you must!"—
And so,—I slowly—
Crumble to the ground.
There is no fright.—
I've played my game.

(1999)

THE WIND

OH!—Listen to the wind
    Swaying thru the trees.—
Hearken!—'tis more than
    A whistling breeze!

Like some magic flute—
    It strangely hums
Its endless tune—
    Thru a billion leaves.

        Whoosh!—Whoosh!
        Whoosh!—Whoosh!

(1994)

TIME

Awesome Time!
No Beginning!
No End!
The Eternal Clock—
Nursing all matter—
From Birth—
To Death—
In Mystery—
Allowing Earthlings,—
Mere Seeds of Chance,—
To witness—
A Moment—
Of its Drama—
In a Flash—
Of Life.

(2001)

Today

We look back from tomorrow—
    And we see today.—
        Since tomorrow may never be—
            Don't let the present slip away.

           Each day seeks
              Its full measure.—
                  It will not be reborn!
                      Go!—Fill it with treasure!

(1973)

TORNADO

(Great Barrington—1995)

Like a thousand thunders from the sky,
    As though the Earth had sinned,—
The swirling, screaming, fingered wind,—
    Swooped downward from on high—
To shatter dream, and hope—and realm.
    The Devil himself was at the helm!
Families torn from home and bed.—
    Twisted wreckage!—Counted dead!
Great was the Fury!—Great was the Cry!
    The people in shock stared into the sky—
Now suddenly Peaceful—where Satan passed by.

(1995)

Tranquility

The Sun held the Globe
In its glowing hands—
And warmed the sands.
It kissed the earth.
The sound
Of bursting seed
And birth—
Of food—
From sea
And ground—
Filled the need—
For Life.

And so—
    In daily rhythm—
        Without end—
            The Sun would bend—
                Ever to the west—
                    To shade the Globe—
                        In a blanket of rest—
                            For the following day.

Thus—
    Tranquility reigned—
        Sans 'civilized' hate—

            All—BEFORE—
                And-AFTER—
                The SPAN—
                    Of MAN!

(2001)

TREASURES

If you seek riches—
    Search your mind.
There you shall
    Great treasures find—
Memories of youth—
    Of childhood play—
Of friends—of kin—
    Of the breath of day.
Think back!—Retrieve!—
    And you will enhance
Moments present—
    And once more dance.
There is no pill!—
    Just ring the bell!
The cost is nil.

(1997)

Treasures In The Round

Hail to thee—Oh Poets—
    Gathered in the Round—
Replete in social graces.
    Listen to the hum—
Oft' subtle and profound—
    Mixing joys and wisdom—
In structured word and sound—
    Such friendly smiling faces—
Sipping—tasting—drinking
    Percolations of the mind—
Stimulating—ever searching
    Treasures more to find.

Go!—Gather 'round Enchanters!
    Seed your thoughts in Rhyme!
Be Bold! ~ Be Planters!
    Harness Fleeting Time!

(2001)

TRUE LOVE IS FOREVER!

Though you are gone—
You are closer still.
I look to the Past.
The Dark is Light!
The Square is Round!
I strain!
Time stands still.
The Past returns.
Fleeting Memories!
I listen.
I hear you.
I see you there!
Ah!—Sweet Memories!
True Love shall forever be.

(2002)

TRY A SMILE

Smile to a stranger—
    Don't be afraid.—
Say Hello to your elders—
    The weary and grayed.—
Be friendly—Be cheerful—
    Hold open that door—
And your heart will fill—
    With joy—and—much more.
      TRY IT NOW!!

(1967)

U.S.A.'s Early West
and The World Today, 2006

When dreams of land so free were told—
They beckoned the eager—young and old—
To grassy plains and the buffalo—
To the wagon cry of "Westward Ho!"

Then,—pioneers were the hardy breed
To expand frontiers and sow their seed.
They scaled those awesome mountain trails
On bloody saddles before trains on rails.
When Indians and Settlers fiercely fought—
When hunters' furs were sold and bought.
When Gun was Law—and Law was naught.
When the blacksmith's clang rang the fired shoe—
When States added stars to our Red—White and Blue!

Those were the days when The Wild West grew!

And Now—we've grown for many years—
In a challenging world of terror and tears.
Our Globe has become a battle ground
Of wars and cries of ethnic sound.

Today—six billion hearts beat a lust for Life!
For Love!—For Hope!—For Family!—
Without Hate!—Without Strife!

Alas!—Dear Lord!—Please Let It Be!

(2006)

VIEWS FROM MY WINDOW

(a painting with words)

Whilst sitting at my window—
    For want of things to do—
I find it oft' relaxes—
    Especially to view
Our Rolling Hills' Condo Square.

These are scenes of Life I want to share:

The Mail Chariot and its cherished news.
    The distant background mountain views.
Young and Old in healthy walk.
    Others just to stop and talk.
Pool drawn children skipping there—
    Vehicle turns that often scare.
I see office, maintenance—and Trustees too—
    Bustling crews with things to do.
The Garbage truck—a monster machine—
    Lifting dumpsters to shake them clean.
Trunks emptied of shoppings galore.

    'Athletes' to tennis and golf—not to ignore.

Elders strolling hand in hand—
    Signs of Love—we understand.
Volunteers off to Tanglewood—
    And other places—to do their good.
I see the hustle and bustle of a Summer's day—
    Including showers that come our way.
The landscape of flower beds—
    The yellows, whites and orange reds.
The setting Sun—its painted rays—
    Draining light from wakeful days.
Add treasures evermore!—And so I thrill—
    To the simple pleasures o'er my window sill.

They are all there—
    In Rolling Hills—
        In our Condo Square!
           Such Joys!
            Priceless views—
              That All can see;—
                All part of the Beauty—
                    Of The Berkshire Symphony.

(2003)

Wake Time!—Cheer-Up!

When you wake up in the morning
And you're feeling kinda blue.
Take that morning shower
And think of things to do.

A new day is dawning.—
It's time to stop that yawning!
You can dress for outdoor walking.—
There's the telephone for talking
To chat about the gossip that is new.
It may even be inviting
To correspond by writing
To a long forgotten friend or two.

Away—all fretting torments!
These are the precious moments!
You're Alive!!
     Now—ain't that Grand?!
Hallelujah!!
     Strike up the Band!!

(1995)

WHEN?

Where is the Old Man of wrinkled face—
Who roamed hither and yon from place to place.
Pointing his long curled walking cane,—
Muttering words that seemed inane?

"Take Heed!—Beware!—The Time grows near!
Mortals,—Forsake All Evil!—Do you hear!?
It's the Devil's song!
'Tis Wrong!—Wrong!—Wrong!
I know your Future!" But,—He wouldn't say.
As he intoned—"BEWARE!" and vanished that day.

(1998)

We Are Each A Book!

There's an old cliche repeated over and over—
"You can't tell a book by its cover".
And we,—like a book,—hold pages within
Unseen,—unread,—even our kin
Cannot fathom the emotions locked in our self—
Be we poor,—or with power and pelf.

Though our covers flash good life and cheer—
Yet deep within lurks that shadow of fear.
And so many old—our bindings well worn—
Carry the Wisdom of Age on pages unborn.

What became of that stirring thought
That succumbed to inactive naught?
Awaken that dormant seed
Once embryo to a telling deed.

Record fond memories of yesterday—
Of joys,—of sorrows,—of fun and play!
Rekindle Life's journey as yet untold—
And your heart's treasures will unfold
Into a memorabilia of history—
For readers—friends and Family.

Too many 'Books' stand silent!
Open them!—Fill full your pages!

Start Now!!

(2002)

YOU SHOULD BE THERE!
IN THE BERKSHIRES

When the violins play
And the drums beat loud,—
When the bodies sway
And the peoples crowd,—
    You should be there—
    In The Berkshires!

Tanglewood!—Oh Tanglewood!
Koussevitsky understood!
Its Theatres and Dance
Oft' rekindles romance
With song in the air.
    You should be there—
    In The Berkshires!

'Neath the stars and the moon—
Oft-times at mid-noon.
On long chairs reclining,—
Picnicing—or dining—
    You'll see them all there—
    In The Berkshires.

With trumpets in heat—
Hear the orchestra's beat—
It's really a treat.
    You should be there—
    In The Berkshires!

For the golfers and walkers—
For the poetry talkers—
For the 'Tennis-Anyone' hawkers—
For the meek and the bold—
For the young and the old,—
    You've got to be there—
    In The Berkshires!

Historical places to explore—
Colleges, musems, lakes and more—
Even memories to restore,—
      You'll enjoy them all there—
      In The Berkshires!

When the colors all change
On the far mountain range—
It's Nature—So strange!
      You'll see it all there—
      In The Berkshires!

When your lungs fill with air—
So fresh—pure and rare—
Nature's gift—everywhere—
      You've got to be there—
      In The Berkshires!

So—Come—One and All!
Do Answer The Call!
      YOU SHOULD BE THERE—
      IN THE BERKSHIRES!

(1994)

POSTSCRIPT

Reading some poems aloud—with emphasis on different words together with tonal control throughout—can vary their thrust.

Try it!

Author

978-0-595-48732-5
0-595-48732-7